HowExpert Guide to Knitting

How to Knit Step by Step, Learn Knitting Skills, and Become a Better Knitter

HowExpert with Jeanne Torrey

For more tips related to this topic, visit HowExpert.com/knitting.

Recommended Resources

- HowExpert.com – Quick 'How To' Guides on All Topics from A to Z by Everyday Experts.
- HowExpert.com/free – Free HowExpert Email Newsletter.
- HowExpert.com/books – HowExpert Books
- HowExpert.com/courses – HowExpert Courses
- HowExpert.com/clothing – HowExpert Clothing
- HowExpert.com/membership – HowExpert Membership Site
- HowExpert.com/affiliates – HowExpert Affiliate Program
- HowExpert.com/jobs – HowExpert Jobs
- HowExpert.com/writers – Write About Your #1 Passion/Knowledge/Expertise & Become a HowExpert Author.
- HowExpert.com/resources – Additional HowExpert Recommended Resources
- YouTube.com/HowExpert – Subscribe to HowExpert YouTube.
- Instagram.com/HowExpert – Follow HowExpert on Instagram.
- Facebook.com/HowExpert – Follow HowExpert on Facebook.

Publisher's Foreword

Dear HowExpert Reader,

HowExpert publishes quick 'how to' guides on all topics from A to Z by everyday experts.

At HowExpert, our mission is to discover, empower, and maximize everyday people's talents to ultimately make a positive impact in the world for all topics from A to Z...one everyday expert at a time!

All of our HowExpert guides are written by everyday people just like you and me, who have a passion, knowledge, and expertise for a specific topic.

We take great pride in selecting everyday experts who have a passion, real-life experience in a topic, and excellent writing skills to teach you about the topic you are also passionate about and eager to learn.

We hope you get a lot of value from our HowExpert guides, and it can make a positive impact on your life in some way. All of our readers, including you, help us continue living our mission of positively impacting the world for all spheres of influences from A to Z.

If you enjoyed one of our HowExpert guides, then please take a moment to send us your feedback from wherever you got this book.

Thank you, and we wish you all the best in all aspects of life.

Sincerely,

BJ Min
Founder & Publisher of HowExpert
HowExpert.com

PS...If you are also interested in becoming a HowExpert author, then please visit our website at HowExpert.com/writers. Thank you & again, all the best!

Table of Contents

Introduction

Each of the projects and steps listed in this book will utilize US size 6 needles and worsted weight yarn. Apart from the dishcloth, the patterns can all use the same exact yarn if desired (though the scarf will need more than the hat and cowl). An outline is included in this section which lists the type of needles and yarn each project will need. Notions are included as well; these are suggested supplies in addition to needles and yarn such as stitch markers and tapestry needles. Stitch markers can be found at major craft chain stores, online, or be made of improvised items such as paper clips. Alternate suggestions are also provided for yarn typically available in chain craft stores and one pair of circular needles could be used for every project in this book. The choice of knitting on flat, circular, or Double Pointed Needles (DPNs) is entirely up to the knitter. Chapter 4 goes over how to knit a swatch, new knitters can make swatches with each different kind of needle to determine their preference.

Pattern Supply Outline

Dishcloth

Needles: US size 6, straight or circular

Yarn: Knit Picks Dishie (alternate: Cookies 'n Cream cotton)

Amount: 50 yards or more

Notions: tapestry needle

Rainbow Scarf

Needles: US size 6, straight or circular

Yarn: Cascade 220 Worsted (alternate: Loops & Threads Impeccable Solids)

Amount: 400 yards or more

Notions: tapestry needle

Cat Ear Hat

Needles: US size 6, circular or DPN

Yarn: Cascade 220 Worsted (alternate: Loops & Threads Impeccable Solids)

Amount: 200 yards or less

Notions: Stitch markers, tapestry needle

Fingerless Gloves

Needles: US size 6, circular or DPN

Yarn: Cascade 220 Worsted (alternate: Loops & Threads Impeccable Solids)

Amount: 200 yards or less

Notions: Stitch markers, tapestry needle, cable needle or extra needle (such as a DPN), and waste yarn

Lace Cowl

Needles: US size 6, circular or DPN

Yarn: Cascade 220 Worsted (alternate: Loops & Threads Impeccable Solids)

Amount: 200 yards

Notions: Stitch markers, tapestry needle

Tip #1: When in doubt, swatch it out! A swatch is a small piece of knitted fabric using the desired needles and yarn to assess the knitter's gauge.

US size 6 needles and Worsted Weight yarn go together like peanut butter and jelly. These cover a broad category of projects and designs. New knitters can go far with a single pair of size 6 needles, especially Circular Needles because they allow knitters to work flat or in the round. The pattern chapters have been hand-picked in order to teach new skills in each project so that, by the end of the book, even the newest knitter will have the confidence to move forward with all the skills necessary to complete any pattern they choose.

Chapter 1: How to Hold the Yarn and Needles

Knitting is a constant dance between yarn, needles, and the knitter. It is a delicate balance between speed and accuracy, where tension is the key to consistency. There are almost as many ways to hold the yarn and needles as there are knitters. This chapter will cover two of the most common methods: English Style and Continental Style. Technically, English Style refers to holding the working yarn (and its tension) in one's dominant hand, while Continental Style refers to holding it in one's non-dominant hand.

In most illustrations available, due to much of the population being right-handed, English Style appears to be holding the yarn in the right hand while Continental Style is holding the yarn in the left. For consistency's sake, this chapter will also utilize the same illustration of English/Right and Continental/Left, however, left-hand-dominant knitters are in the unique situation of choosing whether they want to say they knit English or Continental and nobody would be the wiser!

English Style Knitting

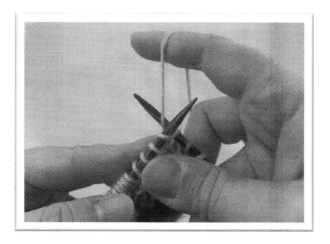

Every knitter holds their yarn and tension slightly differently; there is no right or wrong way to do this. There is a "right" and a "left" way to hold the yarn, however, and that is the main difference between English and Continental style knitting. It is recommended that new knitters attempt holding the working yarn in both hands to determine which is more comfortable for them.

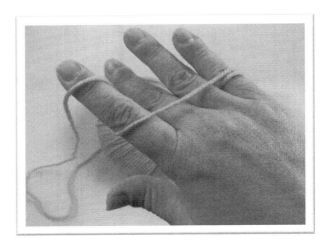

Spreading the tension of the working yarn over the hand is also something that is different for each knitter. Some knitters will wrap the yarn only around the index finger while others will weave it between all their fingers. Most knitters who work in English Style will hold the yarn in their right (dominant) hand. They may feel this gives them more control over the yarn itself or that it is simply more comfortable in their right hand.

Tip #2: There are a variety of videos online of knitters demonstrating their method. Search "How I Knit" to find them on various social media and video platforms.

Holding the needles themselves can vary by knitter as well. Some knitters will manipulate their needles with only a few fingers while others will incorporate their palm to cover a larger area. Beginners may attempt to knit a few stitches with their hands in different positions until they find one that is comfortable for them. Additionally, the way one holds the needles or the yarn while learning to knit does not necessarily have to be permanent. It is entirely possible to learn by using what is comfortable at the time, then later, perhaps after seeing another knitter's method, learn a new one.

Another way of holding the needles that is more common in English style is using a pencil grip on the right needle. The left needle remains stationary in this method with the right needle doing all the manipulation of the yarn. Continental knitters are not excluded from holding the needles in this manner; however, it is a smoother action to knit this way in English style.

Continental Style Knitting

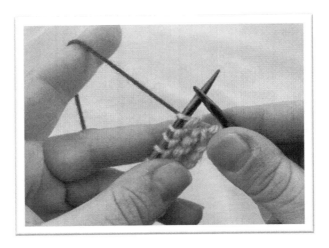

If a knitter is more comfortable using their left (non-dominant) hand to hold the working yarn, they are using the Continental Style. Continental knitters have all the same options for holding the yarn and needles as English Style knitters, they are simply mirrored on the left side. Left-hand dominant or cross-dominant beginners may find that holding the working yarn in the left hand comes more naturally than in the right.

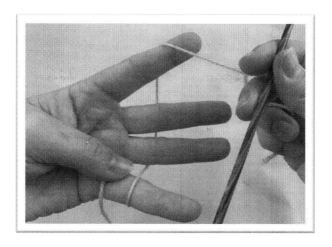

Left-handed or non-dominant knitters rejoice, Continental Style might just be for you! Tension your yarn around your hand or finger in whatever way feels comfortable on your left hand. Some of the fastest knitters in the world use Continental Style.

One benefit that Continental style provides is, when combined with the picking method for creating the stitches (covered in the next chapter), it can be much faster than English style. Many speed knitters hold their yarn in their left hands, even if they are normally right-hand dominant. The reasoning is that yarn placement in the left hand is optimal for creating the stitches with minimal movement. Continental knitters can shift between a knit stitch and a purl stitch (also covered in the next chapter) quickly, making textures, such as ribbing, a breeze.

Tip #3: The fastest knitters in the world are Continental Pickers! Miriam Tegels set the world record with 118 stitches in one minute!

Working with Knitting Needles (English or Continental Style)

Knitters can reference this section later once needles have been chosen and they are ready to begin. Chapter 2 can be referenced for step-by-step instructions on specific stitches.

Basic Steps to Knit with Straight Needles:

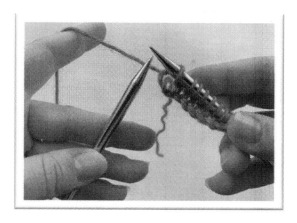

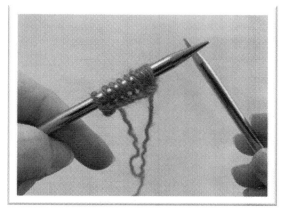

Step 1: Cast on the desired number of stitches. If unsure how to Cast On, choose a method detailed in Chapter 3.

Step 2: Ensure the needle with the cast on row is held in the left hand.

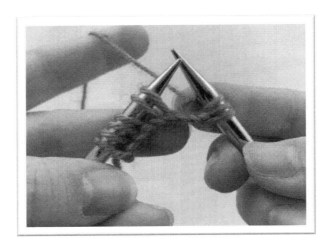

Step 3: Knit or purl the stitches from the left needle to the right needle.

Step 4: Once all stitches have been worked, move the needle with the stitches to the left hand, and repeat Steps 3-4.

Basic Steps to Knit with Circular Needles

These instructions can apply to both the standard size circular needles as well as the short, or "mini", circular needles.

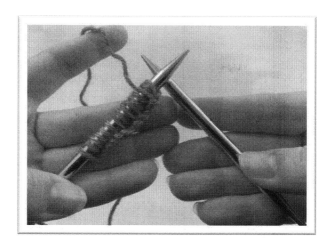

Step 1. Cast on the desired number of stitches.
Optional: Place Beginning of Round (BOR) marker.

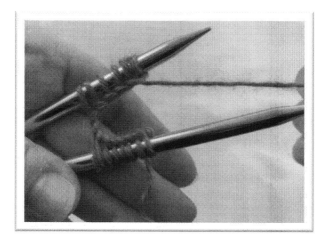

Step 2: Join in the round, being careful not to twist the stitches.

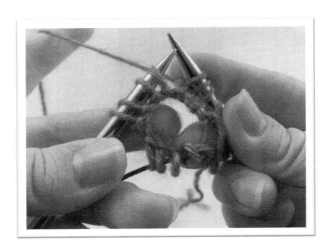

Step 3: Knit or purl all the way across the round.

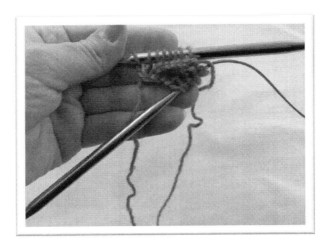

Step 4. Pull the right needle through the work so the left needle goes into the new round.

Step 5: Repeat Step 4.

Basic Steps to Knit with Double Pointed Needles (DPNs)

Step 1: Cast on the desired number of stitches.

Step 2: Split the stitches evenly onto 3-4 DPNs.
Optional: Place the Beginning Of Round (BOR) marker.

Step 3: Join in the round, being careful not to twist the stitches.

Step 4: Using the remaining DPN, knit or purl across the first DPN. The first DPN will now be free of stitches.

Step 5: Using the free DPN, knit or purl across the next DPN.

Step 6: Repeat Step 5.

Picking vs Throwing the Working Yarn

In addition to English Style knitters and Continental Style knitters, there are also Pickers and Throwers. Neither is "right" or "wrong"; as mentioned previously, the most important factor is what is comfortable for the knitter. Most new knitters learn to throw before they learn to pick; the more exaggerated movements of throwing the yarn around the needle is easier to see and understand.

Tip #4: The combination of your knitting style and the way the yarn is made can affect your gauge.

A right-handed knitter, typically shown as English Style, will usually be a thrower automatically due to the nature of knitting from the left needle to the right. Inserting the needle into the stitches on the left side moves the tip away from the working yarn held in the right hand. As a result, the knitter must move the yarn to and around the needle to create the new stitch. However, there are a handful of right-handed knitters who are accomplished pickers by reversing the direction they knit. By going from the right needle to the left, these "backwards" knitters can move the needle to the working yarn with minimal effort.

Meanwhile, the left-handed knitter, commonly shown as Continental Style, has their choice of either picking or throwing without much adjustment on their part. Inserting the right needle into the stitch, the working yarn in the left hand is already close to the tip and the knitter can either move the yarn to the needle or use the needle to "grab" the yarn. Picking is generally considered faster than throwing, in fact, some of the fastest knitters in the world are pickers. A knitter who picks may also have an easier time switching between knit and purl stitches, as it is easier to bring the yarn forward from where the picker holds it.

Tip #5: Experienced knitters, especially Continental Pickers, can knit without looking at their stitches!

Ultimately, knitting should be a relaxing and enjoyable hobby. The focus should be on the knitter being comfortable, not on what is the "right way" or "wrong way" to work through a project. Every pattern can be modified, strict adherence is not a requirement if the knitter is not enjoying the process. Each knitter should find what works for them and adapt any directions or patterns to fit their needs.

Review

- English Style is where knitters hold the working yarn in their dominant (or right) hand.
- Continental Style is where knitters hold the working yarn in their non-dominant (or left) hand.
- Circular needles and DPNs can either knit flat or in the round.
- Straight needles can only knit flat.
- Throwing is bringing the yarn to the needle while working a stitch.
- Picking is bringing the needle to the working yarn while working a stitch.

Chapter 2: Introduction to Fundamental Knitting Stitches

It may seem overwhelming to look at a knitting pattern for the first time and see different abbreviations, symbols, and terms. The goal of this chapter is to break down the most common stitches, and their abbreviations, used by knitters as well as provide a source for future reference. This chapter is not intended as a guide to every knitting stitch available but rather a series of building blocks to help build a solid foundation. Knitting a swatch, or Swatching, is one way that knitters can practice a new stitch without worrying about "messing up". A swatch can be any size, one common size is to Cast On 20 stitches and work the swatch until a specific length or the knitter is comfortable with the new stitch.

Tip #6: Throughout this book, the different stitches and terms will have their accompanying abbreviation in parenthesis to get you used to seeing them.

The Knit Stitch (K)

The first stitch that most new knitters learn is the knit stitch. It is the quintessential stitch in every knitter's arsenal. Each stitch is functionally made up of three parts: the front leg, back leg, and purl bump (top). The purpose of the knit stitch is for legs to form a V-shape and the purl bump to rest behind the stitch above it. When all the purl bumps are on one side of the fabric, this is known as Stockinette Stitch (if the purl bumps

are on the wrong side of the work) or Reverse
Stockinette Stitch (if the bumps are on the right side).
When the purl bumps are on both sides of the work,
this is known as Garter Stitch.

Steps to Work a Knit Stitch:

Step 1: Hold the needle with the Cast On stitches on the
left, the empty needle on the right, and the working
yarn in the back of the work.

Step 2: The leg closest to the knitter is the front leg, insert the right needle into the first stitch (between the front and back legs) from left to right and back to front.

Step 3: Bring the working yarn around the right needle counterclockwise.

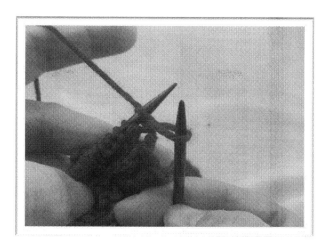

Step 4: Angle the right needle slightly upwards, to better catch the yarn, and pull the yarn through both legs of the stitch. A new stitch has been created and is on the right-hand needle.

Step 5: Carefully slip the "old" stitch, the one that the new stitch was pulled through, off the left needle. This can be scary and that is ok!

Step 6: Repeat Steps 1-5 for the remaining stitches or as the pattern dictates.

The Purl Stitch (P)

The purl stitch, in conjunction with the knit stitch, can contribute to a wide array of textures and patterns. Whether it is used in a Fisherman's Rib stitch or a Seed Stitch, there are a multitude of combinations with which to use the purl and knit stitches together. A purl stitch is essentially a knit stitch that is worked backward. To some knitters, the purl stitch can feel akin to writing with one's non-dominant hand. With a little patience and persistence though, the purl stitch can be mastered and flow just as easily as a knit stitch.

Steps to Work a Purl Stitch

Step 1: Hold the needle with the "live" stitches (the stitches which are ready to be worked) on the left, the empty needle on the right, and the working yarn in the front of the work.

Step 2: The leg closest to the knitter is the front leg; insert the right needle into the first stitch (between the front and back legs) from right to left and back to front.

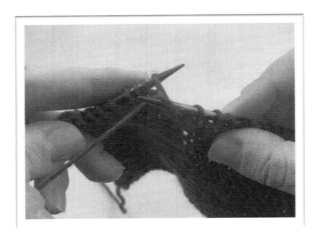

Step 3: Bring the working yarn up, around the right needle counterclockwise, then back down.

Step 4: Angle the right needle slightly upwards, to better catch the yarn, and pull the yarn back through both legs of the stitch. A new stitch has been created and is on the right-hand needle with the purl bump in the front.

Step 5: Carefully slip the "old" stitch, the one that the new stitch was pulled through, off the left needle. This can be scary and that is ok!

Step 6: Repeat Steps 1-5 for the remaining stitches or as the pattern dictates.

Knit 2 Together (K2TOG)

Decreases are used to reduce the number of stitches on the needles. Decreases can make a garment smaller or taper the crown of hats. There are many patterns written that only say "decrease" and not what type of decrease to work. In most cases, especially in older patterns, that decrease is going to be a Knit 2 Together, or K2TOG. The knitter works two stitches together as if they were one, decreasing their row count by 1 stitch and creating a right-leaning effect. This is especially desirable if knit on the left side of a project; the stitches become parallel with the edge of the work.

Steps to Work a K2TOG Stitch

Step 1: Hold the needle with the "live" stitches (the stitches which are ready to be worked) on the left, the empty (or mostly empty) needle on the right, and the working yarn in the back of the work.

Step 2: Insert the right needle into the second stitch from the right (between the front and back legs) from left to right and immediately do the same for the first stitch on the right.

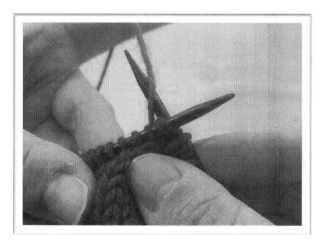

Step 3: Bring the working yarn around the right needle counterclockwise.

Step 4: Angle the right needle slightly upwards, to better catch the yarn, and pull the yarn through both stitches. A single, right-leaning stitch has been created from two stitches.

Step 5: Carefully slip the "old" stitches, the ones that the new stitch was pulled through, off the left needle.

Step 6: Repeat Steps 1-5 as the pattern dictates.

Slip Slip Knit (SSK)

Knit 2 Together's counterpart is the Slip Slip Knit decrease, or SSK. This left-leaning stitch looks lovely on the right side of a project, making the decreases look effortless. Where the K2TOG is knitting 2 stitches as they appear, the SSK involves altering the stitches slightly and then knitting them, essentially, through the back of the loop. Slipping the stitches changes the orientation of the front and back legs on the needle, it twists the stitch before knitting it.

Steps to Work an SSK Stitch

Step 1: Hold the needle with the "live" stitches (the stitches which are ready to be worked) on the left, the empty (or mostly empty) needle on the right, and the working yarn in the back of the work.

Step 2: Slip the first stitch onto the right needle by inserting it as if to knit, then sliding it off the left needle without working it.

Step 3: Repeat Step 2 for the second stitch on the left needle.

Step 4: Insert the left needle into both stitches, left to right, and wrap the working yarn around the right needle counterclockwise.

Step 5: Angle the right needle slightly upwards, to better catch the yarn, and pull the yarn through both

stitches. A single, left-leaning stitch has been created from two stitches.

Step 6: Carefully slip the "old" stitches, the ones that the new stitch was pulled through, off the left needle.

Step 7: Repeat Steps 1-6 as the pattern dictates.

Yarn Over (YO)

The wonderful thing about Yarn Overs is that so many new knitters work them without even realizing it. A Yarn Over is done by wrapping the working yarn around the right needle counterclockwise without having inserted the needle into a stitch first. If a new knitter gets the order of the knit stitch mixed up, for example, if they wrap the yarn, then insert the needle into the next stitch, this can result in several unintentional stitches. However, it can be encouraging for new knitters to learn that they have taught themselves a new stitch with almost no effort! One thing to note, though, is that Yarn Overs do not create a purl bump like many of the other stitches do because it is not working an existing stitch. They also give the appearance of a hole in the work; this is normal and usually the intent of the pattern designer when calling for a Yarn Over.

Steps to Work a YO Stitch

Step 1: Hold the needle with the "live" stitches (the stitches which are ready to be worked) on the left, the empty (or mostly empty) needle on the right, and the working yarn in the back of the work.

Step 2: Wrap the working yarn around the right needle counterclockwise.

Step 3: Move onto the next stitch in the pattern!

Seriously, it is just that easy.

Knit Front and Back (KFB)

If a pattern designer needs to increase the stitch count of a row or round but does not want to create the appearance of a hole left by the Yarn Over, they may use the Knit Front and Back. KFB for short. This increase adds a new stitch by knitting the same stitch twice, once on the front leg and once on the back leg. It is also nearly invisible as an increase in garter stitch, it produces a purl bump on the front and back of the work that blend into the purl ridges almost seamlessly.

Steps to Work a KFB Stitch

Step 1: Hold the needle with the "live" stitches (the stitches which are ready to be worked) on the left, the empty (or mostly empty) needle on the right, and the working yarn in the back of the work.

Step 2: Insert the right needle into the first stitch, left to right and front to back.

Step 3: Wrap the working yarn around the right needle counterclockwise.

Step 4: Pull the needle back through the stitch but do not let the old stitch drop off yet!

Step 5: Insert the right needle into the first stitch again, this time as if to purl, right to left, but keeping the point towards the back.

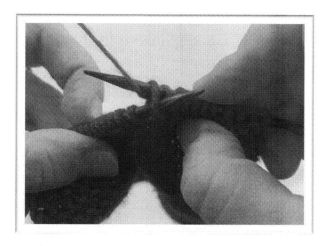

Step 6: Wrap the working yarn around the right needle counterclockwise a second time.

Step 7: Pull the right needle through the stitch and let it drop off the left needle. Two stitches have been knit from one original stitch.

Tip #7: Ravelry.com contains a search feature for Local Yarn Stores based on Zip Code

Every stitch in this chapter will set a new knitter up for success with any pattern they choose to tackle. Knit and Purl are the foundations of working many projects and, especially when combined with the increases and decreases also covered, there should not be too many surprises in the knitting world in terms of new stitches. While the knitter may come across something not mentioned in this chapter such as a PSSO, or Pass Slipped Stitch Over, that decrease method is made up of individual elements that are discussed in this chapter. If there is ever any doubt about how to execute any stitch mentioned in any pattern, the internet (or a Local Yarn Store) has many resources available to assist. Video tutorials are especially helpful for new knitters.

Review

- The knit stitch utilizes the working yarn held to the back and places the purl bump in the back
- The purl stitch utilizes the working yarn held to the front and places the purl bump in the front
- Knit 2 Together is a right-leaning decrease
- Slip Slip Knit is a left-leaning decrease
- Yarn Over is an increase that leaves a hole
- Knit Front and Back is an increase with a purl bump in front

Chapter 3: Starting and Finishing a Project

Both Cast On and Bind Off techniques can be more difficult to master as most projects only require that each be done one time. Knitting a swatch can help familiarize the new knitter with the different methods as well as begin to train muscle memory. Swatching also provides the opportunity to practice weaving in ends, or tails, on different types of stitching. Garter stitch, for example, is easier to hide the ends in than lace.

Tip #8: Knitters use the abbreviation "WIP" online; which stands for Work In Progress.

How to Cast On (CO)

The patterns featured in this book will utilize one of two different cast on methods. A given pattern will use either the Long Tail Cast On or the Knitted Cast On. This chapter, containing detailed step-by-step instructions, can be referenced as needed. The patterns themselves will specify how many stitches to Cast On.

Long Tail Cast On

The Long Tail Cast On has a major benefit of knitting a row of stitches as it goes in addition to being a speedy cast on. Its name is accurate; you will need a long tail to achieve this cast on if you want to get it right the first time. There is a relatively easy and fast method to determine how much length your tail will need without a ruler and leaving enough left over to weave in at the end.

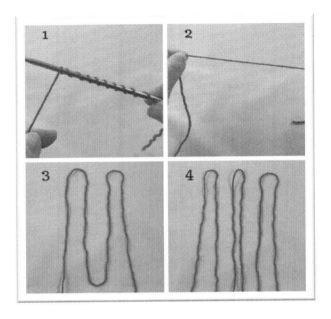

Setup for Long Tail Cast On: Using either a pair of circular needles or a set of Double Pointed Needles, wrap the yarn around needle[1] ten times. Take the length of yarn off the needle[2] and use it to measure more sections of yarn[3] by 10s until you are close to your cast on number[4].

Step 1: Make a slip knot in the estimated section where the last cast on stitch would be and place it on one of the needles.

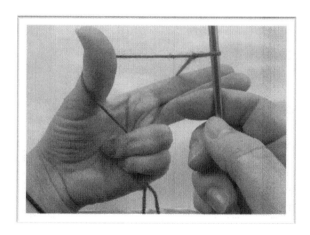

Step 2: Holding the Needle in your right hand, wrap the working yarn around the back of your left index or middle finger and the tail around the back of your thumb. Secure the yarn if you can with your left middle, ring, and pinky fingers.

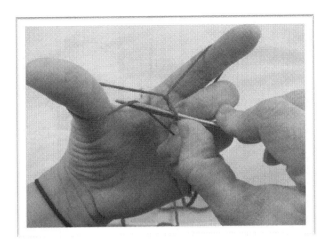

Step 3: Bring the Needle down to the outside of the loop on your thumb and bring it under the yarn.

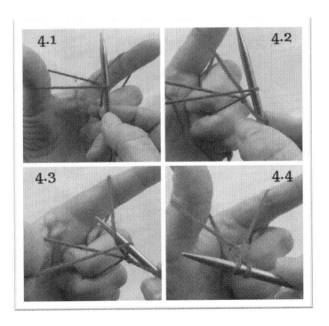

Step 4: Move the Needle up and come around to the outside of the loop on your index or middle finger[4.1]. Bring it down through the loop and catch the inside "leg"[4.2-3], pulling it down between the legs of the loop on your thumb[4.4].

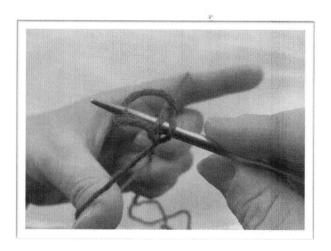

Step 5: Return the Needle to the starting position and use your thumb or right hand to pull the tail (closest to you) tight. There are now two stitches on the Needle.

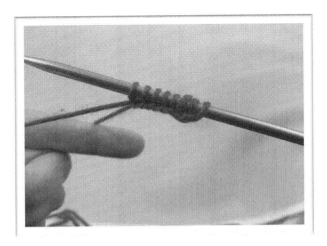

Step 6: Repeat Steps 1-5 until you have Cast On the desired number of stitches.

The Long Tail Cast On is now complete!

Knitted Cast On

The Knitted Cast On is a classic and with good reason. This cast on is not as stretchy as some of its counterparts, however it is remarkably durable and holds up well over time. For projects that are worn frequently, the Knitted Cast On is the perfect choice.

Setup for the Knitted Cast On: This cast on can be done with either a pair of circular needles or two Double Pointed Needles. The working yarn is held for tension as if you are knitting.

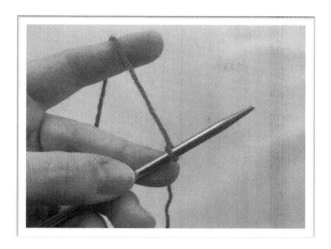

Step 1: Make a slip knot on the Left Needle.

Step 2: Insert the Right Needle through the slip knot, right to left and front to back.

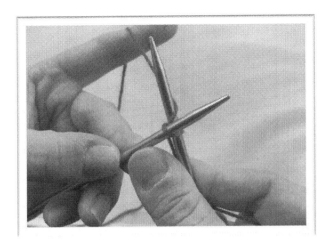

Step 3: Wrap the working yarn around the Right Needle

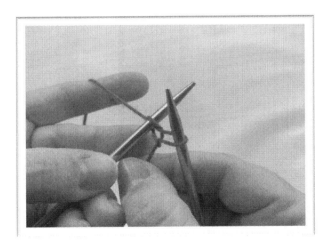

Step 4: Pull the Right Needle back through the slip knot

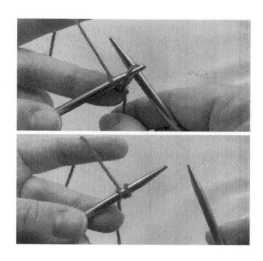

Step 5: Place the loop from the Right Needle onto the Left Needle. There are now two stitches on the Left Needle.

Step 6: Insert the Right Needle between the two stitches on the Left Needle and wrap the working yarn around the needle.

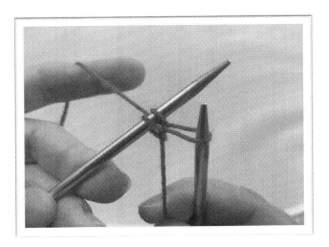

Step 7: Pull the Right Needle back through the stitches and place the loop from the Right Needle onto the Left Needle. There are now three stitches on the Left Needle.

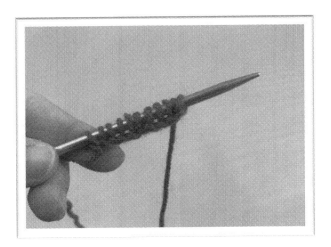

Step 8: Repeat Steps 6 and 7 by inserting the Right Needle between the first and second stitches on the Left

Needle until the desired number of stitches have been cast on.

The Knitted Cast On is complete!

Backwards Loop Cast On

This Cast On is used almost exclusively mid-project to make up for either separating stitches, filling a gap, or to replace stitches that were bound off. This method should be used sparingly and is not a stable choice at the beginning of a project. Later in this book it will be used in the fingerless gloves pattern once the thumb gusset has been moved onto waste yarn.

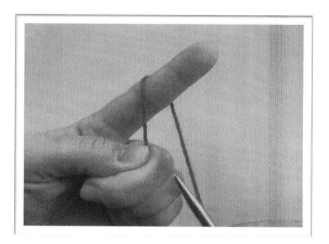

Step 1: Wrap the working yarn around your left finger counterclockwise. This forms two "legs", the working yarn should be the right leg and the tail end should be the left.

Step 2: Insert your right needle back to front and left to right through the left leg on your finger.

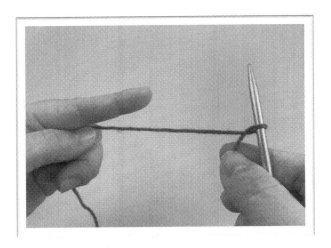

Step 3: Pull your finger out of the loop and tighten it on the needle by pulling the tail

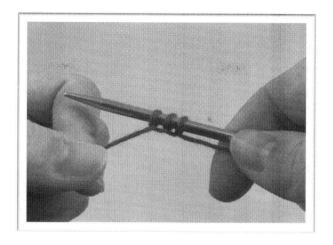

Step 4: Repeat Steps 1-3 as necessary to cast on the number of stitches desired.

The Backwards Loop Cast On is complete!

How to Bind Off (BO)

Tip #9: Though most knitters use the term "Bind Off" for the action of finishing a project, the term "FO" or Finished Object is used after it is completed.

Knitted Bind Off

The Knitted Bind Off is commonly the first bind off a new knitter learns because of how similar it is to the knit stitch. However, the name is a bit of a misnomer as it could also be called the Purled Bind Off or Ribbed Bind Off. The knitter has the choice of either purling or knitting, or both, while working the bind off.

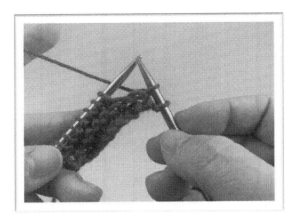

Step 1: Knit/Purl 2 stitches.

Step 2: Pass the first stitch over the second stitch and off the needle. The first stitch has been bound off.

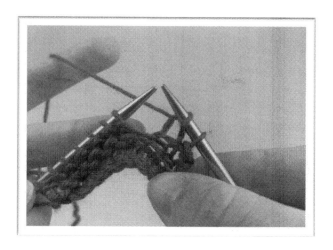

Step 3: Knit/Purl 1 stitch.

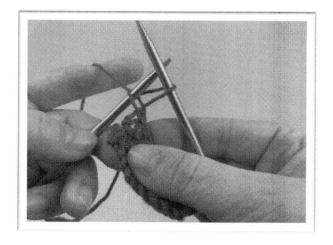

Step 4: Repeat Steps 2-3 until there is 1 stitch remaining.

Step 5: Knit/Purl the remaining stitch, then cut the yarn and pull it through the last stitch to tighten.

The knitted bind off is complete.

JSSBO: Jeny's Surprisingly Stretchy Bind off

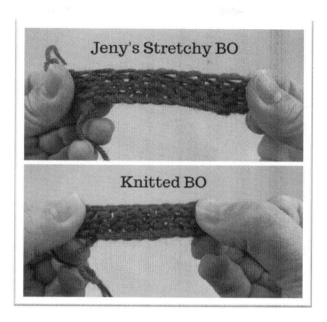

In the fall of 2009, Knitty.com published a new bind off designed by Jeny Staiman and the world of knitters rejoiced! Abbreviated as JSSBO, Jeny's Surprisingly Stretchy Bind Off became the go-to bind off for many a sock knitter because it makes an elastic edge perfect for cuffs.

<u>Knit Stitch Instructions:</u>

Step 1: Knit 1, reverse Yarn Over, Knit 1.

Step 2.1: Insert needle into both the YO and the first knit stitch.

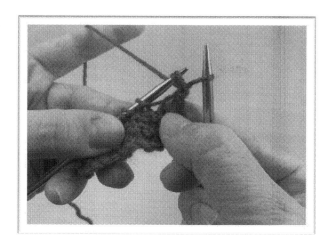

Step 2.2: Pass both the YO and first knit stitch over the second knit stitch.

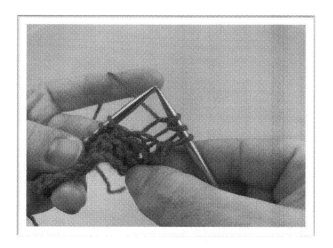

Step 3: Reverse YO, knit 1.

Step 4: Repeat Steps 2-3 until 1 stitch remains.

Step 5: Cut the yarn and pull it through the last stitch to tighten.

Purl Stitch Instructions:

Step 1: Purl 1, YO (in the normal direction), Purl 1.

Step 2: Insert needle into both the YO and the first purl stitch, pass both over the second purl stitch.

Step 3: YO, purl 1.

Step 4: Repeat Steps 2-3 until 1 stitch remains.

Step 5: Cut the yarn and pull it through the last stitch to tighten.

JSSBO is complete.

Three Needle Bind Off

This bind off is worked almost as a graft, however, it is still considered a type of knitted bind off. The Three Needle Bind Off requires an additional needle, ideally smaller in size than the needles used on the project, equal or one size up will do in a pinch. Whether the extra needle is a DPN, a straight needle, or one of a pair of circular needles, this bind off will still be achievable.

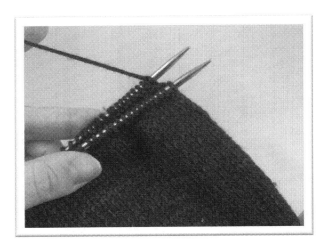

Step 1: Evenly distribute the remaining stitches onto two needles and hold them parallel.

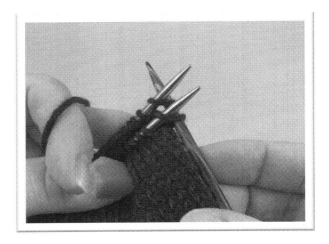

Step 2: Insert the third needle knit-wise (left to right, front to back—as if to Knit) into the first stitch on the front needle, then knit-wise into the first stitch back needle.

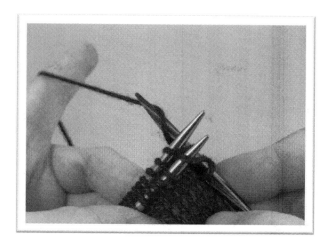

Step 3: Wrap the yarn around the third needle as if to knit, pull the needle through both stitches and allow both to fall off their respective needles.

Step 4: Repeat Steps 2-3. There are now two stitches on the third needle.

Step 5: Lift the first stitch on the third needle over the second stitch, as if doing a Knitted Bind Off.

Step 6: Repeat Steps 2-3 and 5 until all stitches but one are bound off.

Step 7: Pull the yarn through the last stitch.

The three needle bind off is complete.

How to Weave in Ends

Weave as You Go

Many knitters opt to weave their tails in as they work through the project. This is especially efficient when working with stripes and there are multiple ends of multiple colors. Addressing the ends prior to finish the socks is an excellent way to avoid a headache later. Doing the ends sooner rather than later means there is one less thing in the way of wearing the finished socks.

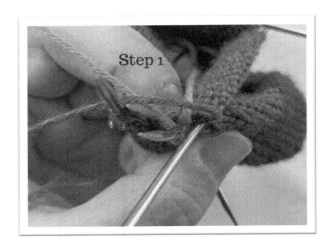

Step 1: Work the first 2-3 stitches in the new color, new round, or new row with the working yarn.

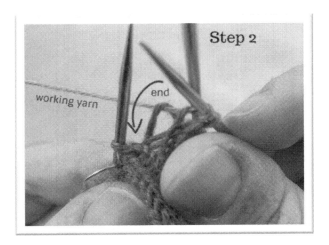

Step 2: On the wrong side of the fabric (inside of the sock), lay the tail to be woven in across the top of the working yarn right to left.

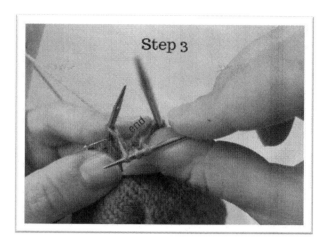

Step 3: Work the next stitch in pattern, but do not catch the tail, allow the working yarn and new stitch to simply hold it in place on the back of the work.

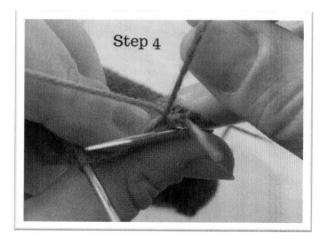

Step 4: Lay the tail across the top of the working yarn, this time left to right.

Step 5: Repeat Steps 2-4 until the tail has been woven behind 8-10 stitches.

Step 6: **Optional** - If planning to block the project, as described in Chapter 13, do not cut the remaining length of tail until after blocking to allow for any additional ease provided by the yarn relaxing.

Medium/Long Ends

When patterns mention how long of a tail to leave, this is generally an estimation erring on the side of caution. Two inches? Six inches? Most of the time, if the tail is only going to be sewn in later, eyeballing 3-4 inches is perfectly acceptable. If the tail needs to be used to graft something closed, such as a toe or heel, then substantially more yarn is necessary. Once a knitter has finished a few projects, they have an idea of about how much tail to leave themselves to weave in at the end.

Step 1: Thread the end through the eye of a tapestry needle.

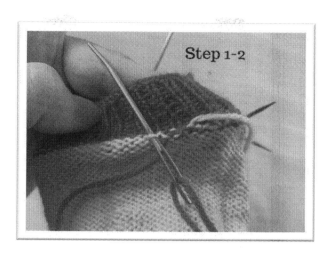

Step 2: On the wrong side of the fabric, the inside of the sock, weave the tapestry needle through the back of the stitches in one direction.

Step 3: Weave the tapestry needle through the back of the stitches in the opposite direction. Ensure the woven tail is not visible from the outside of the sock.

Step 4: Repeat Steps 2-3 as necessary then cut or trim the remaining length of tail. If blocking the project, do not trim the tail until after blocking.

Short Ends

Short ends happen. Whether an end is snipped too early, blocking stretched the fabric out, or a Long Tail Cast On turned out not to be so long after all, there is always a way to address a short end. This method may take some practice, and there are special needles available with larger eyes, but it is possible with a standard tapestry needle and some creative angling.

Step 1: Weave the empty tapestry needle through the backs of stitches near the short end of yarn. The eye of the needle should land near the end to be woven in.

Step 2: Gently thread the short tail through the eye of the tapestry needle, keeping the point woven through the backs of stitches.

Step 3: Pull the tapestry needle through the stitches. The tail may not weave all the way through the selected stitches, but that is ok, the end is now secure.

Step 4: **Optional** – If blocking the project, do not trim any excess off the short end until after blocking is complete.

Tip #10: Work short swatches in order to practice different Cast On and Bind Off methods!

Many knitters, both new and experienced, are often in a rush to finish a project to wear it, gift it, or just show it off. Good finishing techniques take practice and patience, like most other skills. Finishing a project is what will help give it that professional and polished look. Likewise, using an appropriate cast on for a project will help provide a solid foundation as the project is worked. The body of a project may look stunning, but if a cast on or bind off is too loose/tight, or loose ends are coming unraveled, that can negatively affect the whole piece. While a cast on or bind off is only one element of a pattern, they are crucial to the fit of a garment and an ill-fitting garment may not be comfortable. Taking time to really practice, as well as having patience in finishing techniques, will elevate a finished project to another level.

Review

- Long Tail Cast On knits a row as it is cast on, estimated yarn length is required.
- Knitted Cast On is less stretchy but holds its shape over time.
- Knitted Bind Off is a firm bind off with little stretch.
- JSSBO is extremely stretchy but uses more yarn than a traditional BO.
- Three Needle Bind Off is a method of grafting that knits two sides together.
- Weaving in Ends is done at the end of a project, so the yarn doesn't unravel.

Chapter 4: How to Read a Knitting Pattern

There are knitters who inherently understand the construction of a garment and can whip up projects without looking at a single pattern. For the rest of us, there are thousands of patterns available on the internet, at the library, or at local yarn and craft stores. Other knitters are also a valuable resource; before patterns were written they were passed down verbally through the generations. Modern patterns often come either written, charted, or a combination of the two.

Tip #11: If you have trouble understanding a pattern, check Ravelry.com's online forum to see if anyone else had the same issue or if the designer has written any clarifications.

Written Patterns

A written pattern can be anything from a few sentences to several pages. Some designers go into thorough detail while others leave room for imagination and interpretation. This section will break down several elements commonly included in modern written patterns.

Materials and Notions

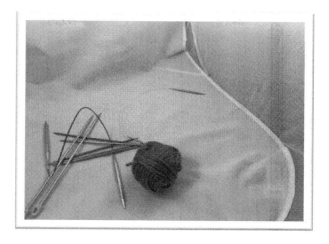

Most patterns will give knitters a list of items needed to complete the project. They will list the amount and weight of yarn, the recommended needle size, and any additional tools—or notions—required. The final needle size will vary depending on the knitter's gauge, which changes person to person. Other notions can include stitch markers to indicate separate sections of stitches, cable needles for helping achieve cable stitches, or tapestry needles for weaving in ends.

Gauge

A common suggestion for needle size in patterns will include the phrase "[...] or the size needed to obtain gauge". Gauge is a combination of the yarn weight, needle size, and knitter's tension on the yarn. The method for obtaining a knitter's gauge with the specific yarn and needle size is to knit a gauge swatch. Typically, a gauge swatch will be in the stitch pattern used for most of the project, such as in stockinette, garter, or in the round. An example of a gauge requirement for a pattern might look like:

18 stitches and 22 rows per 4 inches in stockinette

The way to determine what combination of needle size with the specified yarn will achieve gauge would be to knit a swatch in stockinette that is at least 4 inches wide and tall. A "recipe" for a gauge swatch is included next and it may seem like a lot of work to do before jumping into a project. Sometimes it is more work than a knitter feels like doing, however, in garments gauge is crucial to get correct otherwise it might negatively affect the final fit.

How to Knit a Gauge Swatch in Stockinette*

*To knit the swatch in garter stitch, substitute all purl stitches for knit stitches

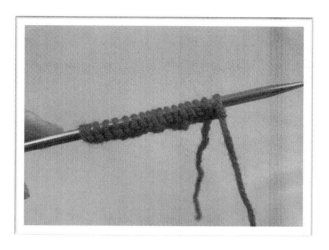

Step 1: Cast on (N+4) stitches, where N is the number of stitches specified in the gauge statement (ex: 18 stitches).

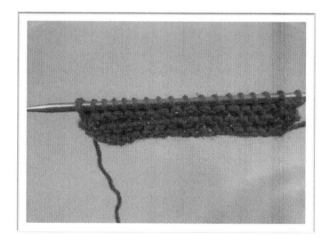

Step 2: Knit 5 rows, resulting in 2-3 garter ridges

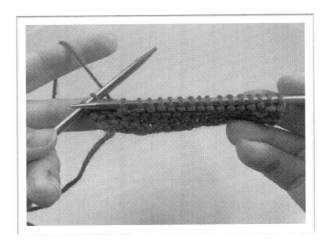

Step 3: Knit 2 stitches, Purl across to the last 2 stitches, Knit the last 2 stitches

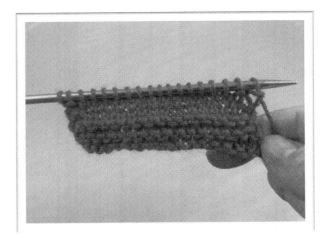

Step 4: Knit across

Step 5: Repeat Steps 3-4 until the specified number of rows or length (ex: 3in) has been reached

Step 6: Using a measuring tape, gauge ruler, or regular ruler, measure the number of stitches and rows in the specified length.

If there are MORE stitches/rows than specified, repeat Steps 1-6 with a larger needle size (go up by one size at a time if possible). If there are FEWER stitches/rows than specified, repeat Steps 1-6 with a smaller needle size. "Getting gauge" is less crucial for projects where fit will not be an issue, such as blankets, scarves, or wraps.

Sizes

When a pattern has multiple sizes, such as for a sweater, instructions for the individual sizes could get mixed up easily. One solution for this is to use a method of separation within the same line. For example, the beginning of the pattern might state:

Sizes included in this pattern are S(M,L)

S is Small, M is Medium, and L is Large but pay attention to the punctuation and special characters in addition to the order of the letters. S is outside the parenthesis; M is the first letter on the inside and L is the last letter. By setting up this method of separation, the designer is making it easier for the knitter to visually distinguish which size is which for later instructions. Cast on and setup row instructions would look something like this:

Cast on 72(84, 96) stitches, join in the round and knit for 10(13, 16) inches.

If working the Small size, the knitter would cast on 72 stitches and knit for 10 inches. Likewise, Medium would cast on 84 stitches and knit for 13 inches while Large is cast on 96 stitches and knit for 16 inches.

If a pattern is covering an even larger array of sizes, such as infant to adult, or increments of height in inches or centimeters, it's not unusual to see multiple methods of separation to include parenthesis, brackets, and bolds. Such as:

Size included in this pattern are 2, 4, 6, **8, 10, 12**(14, 16, 18, **20, 22, 24**)[26, 28, 30, **32, 34, 36**]

When encountering a pattern such as this, it is recommended to highlight the size being knit all the way through the pattern for even easier visual reference. A little bit of prep time at the beginning will save a lot of headache along the way.

Common Abbreviations and Instructions

Most patterns will abbreviate stitches in the directions and provide corresponding definitions. Once the knitter is familiar with the abbreviations, the shorthand directions are typically appreciated, especially in larger projects. The abbreviations help both the designer use space efficiently for minimal pagers and the knitter who will have to track their progress within the pattern.

While there may be slight variations in how designers abbreviate stitch names, there are some that are generally agreed upon:

K	Knit	SL	Slip Stitch
P	Purl	KFB	Knit Front and Back

YO	Yarn Over	M1L	Make 1 (stitch) Left leaning
K2TOG	Knit 2 Together	M1R	Make 1 (stitch) Right leaning
SSK	Slip Slip Knit	CO	Cast On
RS	Right Side	BO	Bind Off
WS	Wrong Side	PSSO	Pass Slipped Stitch Over
PM	Place Marker	Rep	Repeat

The patterns in the later chapters of this book are not abbreviated for the sake of the beginning knitter. If they were to contain abbreviations, however, they would read like this:

<u>Dishcloth</u>
Setup Row (WS): Using the knitted CO, CO4
Row 1 (RS): K across
Row 2 (WS): K across
Row 3 (RS): *K2, YO, K across; rep from * until desired width is reached
Row 4 (WS): *K1, K2TOG, YO, K1, K2TOG, K across; rep from * until 6 stitches remain
Row 5 (RS): K1, K2TOG, YO, K1, K2TOG, K across
Row 6 (WS): K1, K2TOG, YO, K2TOG, K across
Row 7 (RS): K1, K2TOG, K
Row 8 (WS): K2TOG, K
Row 9 (RS): K2TOG
Row 10 (WS): YO, pass K2TOG over YO, cut working yarn and pull the YO through with the needle

A variation on the Repeat instruction can also include parenthesis (), where the stitches to be repeated will be inside. The designer may write a row of instructions as:

In this example, the (YO, K) instruction is repeated three times before moving onto the Knit 3.

Patterns with Charts

18	17	16	15	14	13	12	11	10	9	8	7	6	5	4	3	2	1	
•	•	•	•	•	•	•	•	•	•	•	•	•	•	•	•	•	•	4
∕	∕	∕		U		U		U		U		U		U	∕	∕	∕	3
																		2
																		1
18	17	16	15	14	13	12	11	10	9	8	7	6	5	4	3	2	1	

Created on **chart-minder.com**

While written patterns may be efficient for less complicated projects, charted patterns allow a designer to convey a lot of information in a minimal amount of space. Charts are a visual representation of the texture as well as the individual stitches. Few charted patterns have only their charts and little else by way of instruction. Many designers will include written cast on and setup rows prior to having knitters begin the chart(s). When using multiple charts in their patterns, designers will indicate what order they should be followed and whether each chart requires any setup rows beforehand.

Tip #12: An easy way to track which row you're on in a chart is either to have a physical copy and use a ruler as a guide, or download the pattern to an app that allows for highlights.

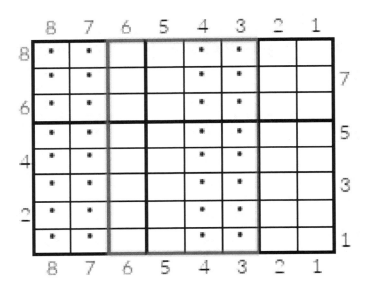

Created on **chart-minder.com**

Typically, a chart is read from right to left, bottom to top with each square representing a stitch and numbers labeling each row. A chart for a flat pattern will be read right to left for odd numbered rows and left to right for even numbered rows. If there is a section that should be repeated (the charted equivalent of *rep from* *) it will be highlighted or outlined. Symbols on charts are even less standardized than abbreviations but designers will include a key to decipher each one.

☐	Most commonly, the knit stitch is identified in a chart as a blank square on the right side. There is a variation in this use when knitting flat; the blank square is then used to indicate a Purl stitch on the wrong side.
⊡	The Purl stitch is identified typically as a dot in the middle of a square on the right-side rows. Like the blank square being a Purl on the wrong side, a dot on the wrong side when knitting flat indicates a Knit stitch. The dot represents the Purl bump being visible on the right side.
⊙	An open circle in the middle of a square represents a Yarn Over. Since there is no Purl bump with a YO, this symbol is usually the same on the right side or wrong side.
⊘	A right-leaning slash represents the K2TOG because it is a right-leaning decrease. This symbol is typically the same on both right and wrong sides.
⊗	A left-leaning slash represents the SSK because it is a left-leaning decrease. This symbol is typically the same on both right and wrong sides.

Other variations in chart symbols can include either a gray square or an area of unlined squares to represent no stitch. This is more commonly seen in charts at the beginning of a set of increases or towards the end of a set of decreases to allow the charts to remain an XY grid and include all stitches.

Tip #13: Another way to track which row you're on is with a Row Counter; this small notion allows you to turn or slide numbers incrementally as you work through the pattern. If you put it down and come back, you'll easily see which row you're on!

If a knitter comes across a pattern that is long and intimidating, mentally breaking it down into sections— if not already written in sections—will help it be more "digestible". One mantra to remember could be "How do you eat an elephant? One bite at a time." Every pattern should be taken "one bite at a time", with the focus on what the next step, row, or round is, rather than ALL the work that has not been completed yet. It is advisable to read the pattern start to finish before working the cast on, and look up stitch definitions or tutorials before they are needed. However, many knitters opt to skip this step entirely or only read a few lines ahead. While working with a physical pattern, a knitter may cover up any future sections so only the current and past rows are visible. If the pattern is digital, some knitters scroll down to cover future sections and focus on the current ones. There is no wrong way to read a pattern, and if something feels "too long", break it down into smaller steps and focus on those. Even the most complicated patterns can be worked this way.

Review

- Patterns will include a Materials or Notions section that will give the knitter an idea of what type of yarn to get and what size needles to start with.
- Gauge is a combination of yarn size, needle size, and knitter's tension.
- Gauge is more important when it comes to the fit of garments and less important for things like accessories (scarves, blankets, shawls, etc).
- When patterns come in multiple sizes, designers will consolidate instructions but provide a method of distinguishing those instructions between each size. Ex: S(M,L)
- There is no real standardization for abbreviations and charts, however, most designers will include a key for what they use in their pattern.

Chapter 5: How to Knit in the Round

Straight needles allow knitters to work back and forth for "flat knitting". Blankets, scarves, curtains, table runners, and dishcloths can all be knit flat on straight needles. However, when a circle or tube is required of the fabric, that is what is known as knitting "in the round". Knitting in the round is accomplished using either Double Pointed Needles (DPNs) or Circular Needles.

Tip #14: Knitting in the round has been around for centuries; the first known pair of knitted socks was uncovered in Egypt and is about 1,700 years old.

Detailed Double Pointed Needle (DPN) Steps

Double Pointed Needles allow stitches to slide on and off both ends as opposed to straight needles, which have stoppers on one end. DPNs have been used for centuries to knit round pieces or tubes, especially socks. Stitches are evenly distributed on three or four DPNs with an extra needle free to begin knitting. The new stitches are transferred to the free needle, which then incorporates that needle as part of the group holding the stitches and freeing up a different needle to repeat the process all the way around. DPNs allow for knitting extremely small tubes with few stitches, such as baby or doll socks, though some beginners may find them a bit challenging to work with at first.

Tip #15: If metal Double Pointed Needles are too finicky and stitches keep sliding off, try a set of Bamboo DPNs. Bamboo provides more resistance than metal and will "grip" the stitches more.

Step 1: Using two DPNs, cast on the specified number of stitches using the chosen method called for in the pattern.

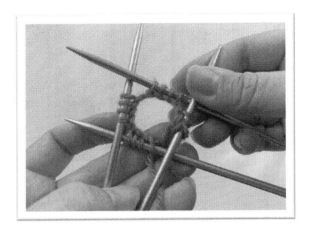

Step 2: As evenly as possible, distribute the stitches between all but one of the DPNs. This may be across three or four DPNs depending on the set of needles and size of the project.

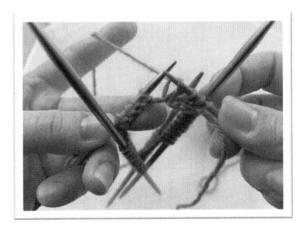

Step 3: Ensure the cast on edge is straight on the needles and not twisted, use the working yarn to knit (or purl as required) across the first needle with the free needle, joining the work in the round.

Step 4: Using the needle that is now free of stitches, knit across the second needle.

Step 5: Repeat Step 4 until all needles have been worked once. A single round has been completed. Repeat previous steps as necessary to follow the pattern.

Tip #16: If DPNs are still a bit difficult to work with in the round, practice knitting swatches in the round. A circular swatch provides a low-stress method of practice because any mistakes won't be in the finished project.

Detailed Circular Needle Steps

Circular Needles are a relatively new invention in the field of knitting, having only been around for about one hundred or one hundred fifty years. They are two needles connected by a cable which can be made up of plastic, metal, nylon, or other material. Working with a set of Circular Needles is almost the same as working with DPNs, if the Circular Needles acted like one long, flexible Double Pointed Needle. Only the two needles are required to knit the active stitches while the cable holds the rest, whereas when working with DPNs other needles hold the non-active stitches. Circular Needles, or "circs" as they are known colloquially, allow for both small and large diameter projects in the round as well as flat knitting. Long cable needles are excellent for large flat projects such as full-size blankets or big shawls.

Tip #17: Some companies, such as Knit Picks or Knitter's Pride, make what are called "Interchangeable Circular Needle" sets. This is where the knitter can swap out the needles without losing any of the stitches on the cable.

Note: The following steps should be followed if the Circular Needle cable being used is short enough to knit in the round comfortably. If the cable is too long, please move on to the next section, Magic Loop Steps.

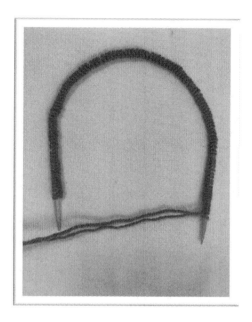

Step 1: Using a set of Circular Needles, cast on the specified number of stitches using the chosen method called for in the pattern.

Step 2: Ensure the cast on edge is straight and not twisted, use the working yarn to knit (or purl as required) the first stitch cast on, joining the work in the round.

Step 3: Knit (or purl as required) across the rest of the stitches, one round has been worked.

Step 4: Place a stitch marker if needed and continue working in the round as necessary to follow the pattern.

Tip #18: Some interchangeable needle sets also allow knitters to connect multiple cables between the needles, which helps accommodate even the largest of projects.

Magic Loop Steps

Sometimes a project is not enough stitches to comfortably fit all the way around a Circular Needle. Perhaps it is a smaller project, or the cable of the needle is too long but the knitter would still prefer to use Circular Needles. The Magic Loop method (and its counterpart the Traveling Loop) takes advantage of the flexibility of Circular Needles by pulling the excess cable out at the sides of the work. The stitches are divided in half by loops of extra cable coming out at the beginning of the round and halfway through.

Step 1: Using a set of Circular Needles, cast on the specified number of stitches using the chosen method called for in the pattern.

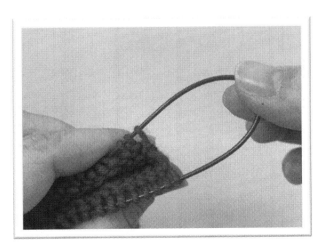

Step 2: Find the halfway point of the stitches and pull the cable all the way through this point. Each set of stitches should be up against its respective needle.

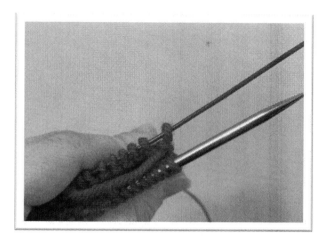

Step 3: Ensure the cast on ridge is straight and not twisted, pull the needle with the working yarn out of the stitches, leaving about half of the excess cable in the first loop. This will be the right-hand needle.

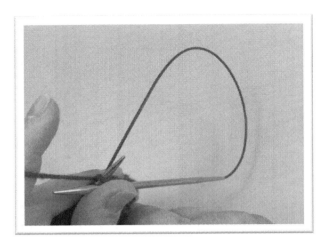

Step 4: Create a second loop with the needle that was pulled out. There should be two loops with the cable now, one on the right and one on the left.

Step 5: Bring the first half of stitches onto the left-hand needle and Knit (or purl as required) across the first set of stitches to the first loop.

Step 6: Turn the work and pull the free needle into the second set of stitches, this is now the left-hand needle.

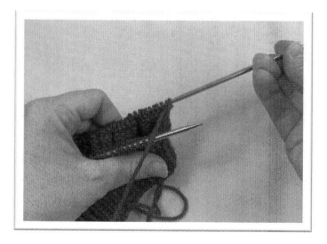

Step 7: Pull the back needle out of the stitches and create a second loop again; this is now the right-hand needle.

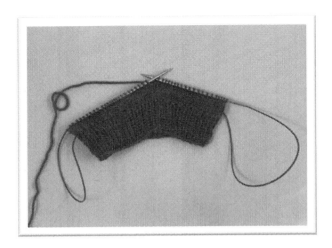

Step 8: Knit across the second set of stitches. The first round has been worked.

Step 9: Repeat Steps 5-8 and continue working in the round as specified by the pattern.

Traveling Loop Steps

Traveling Loop is executed the same way as Magic Loop when the cable is too long for the stitches to fit comfortably around but too short to form two loops. Rather than having a loop halfway through the stitches, Traveling Loop has a single loop at the beginning/end of the round. This method may also be utilized if the cable is long enough for two loops, but the knitter prefers to have one loop, however that single loop will be larger and could be more difficult to handle than two.

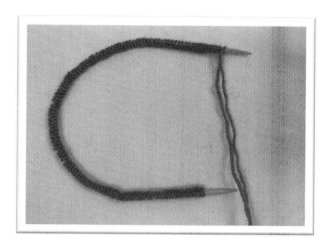

Step 1: Using a set of Circular Needles, cast on the specified number of stitches using the chosen method called for in the pattern.

Step 2: Ensure the cast on ridge is straight and not twisted, pull the needle with the working yarn out of the stitches. This will be the right-hand needle.

Step 3: Create a loop with the needle that was pulled out. There will only be one loop which is at the beginning/end of the round.

Step 4: Bring the stitches onto the left-hand needle and Knit (or purl as required) across the round.

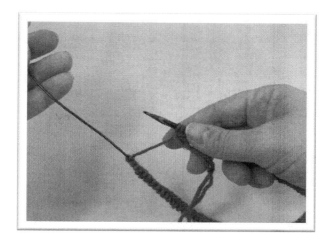

Step 5: Upon reaching the end of the round, pull the left-hand needle back into the stitches and form another loop with the right-hand needle.e

Step 6: Repeat Steps 4-5 and continue working in the round as specified by the pattern.

Tip #19: Many sock knitters enjoy working with "mini circs", a pair of short tipped and short cabled needles that are exactly the right size to knit one sock in the round without DPNs or using Magic Loop.

Practicing knitting in the round or working a tubular swatch will help immensely with giving a new knitter the confidence to use either DPNs or circular needles. It is hardly fun to work on a piece that is going to be ripped out at the end such as with swatches, however, there is significantly less stress to have every stitch look "perfect" on a swatch. Mistakes can be made, lessons can be learned, and the knitter can move on without also trying to correct the mistake. Knitting in the round can be used for everything from hats, sleeves, sweaters, socks, pants, even start shaped blankets. This is a valuable tool in the knitter's "toolbox" and practicing will help ease the stress of learning.

Review

- Double Pointed Needles allow stitches to slide on/off both ends.
- Bamboo DPNs can provide more friction than metal, preventing stitches from slipping off accidentally.
- Circular Needles can knit flat or in the round.
- The Magic Loop method can be used when the cable is too long for the stitches to fit comfortably around a pair of Circular Needles.
- Magic Loop pulls the excess cable out into two loops on either side of the project.
- The Traveling Loop method can be used when the cable is too short for two loops.
- Traveling Loop pulls the excess cable out into one loop at the beginning/end of the round.

Chapter 6: Knitting a Dishcloth

As a first project, it is difficult to find a better one than the classic dishcloth. Knit in cotton, worsted weight yarn, it is satisfyingly quick to work up several of these functional pieces. Cotton yarn is surprisingly durable, and these dishcloths will even be able to undergo many trips through the washing machine. This pattern is an excellent first project because it covers a simple Cast On, the knit stitch, a basic increase (the Yarn Over), one of the most common decreases (Knit 2 Together), and a quick Bind Off. The quick pattern also gives a satisfying sense of accomplishment early on, encouraging the new knitter to take their skills forward.

Dishcloth Supplies

Needles: US size 6, straight or circular

Yarn: Knit Picks Dishie (alternate: Cookies 'n Cream cotton)

Amount: 50 yards or more

Cast On

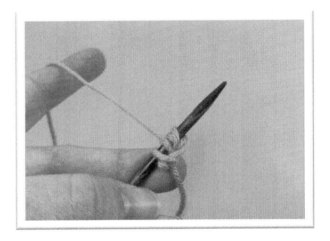

Step 1: Cast On (CO) 4 stitches with the Knitted Cast On method described in Chapter 2.

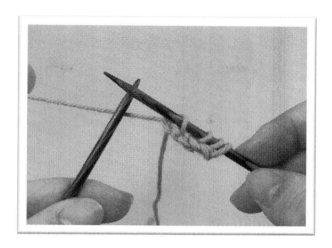

Step 2: Knit across the 4 stitches, turn the work, and switch the hands holding the needles (the one with the stitches should wind up in the left hand)

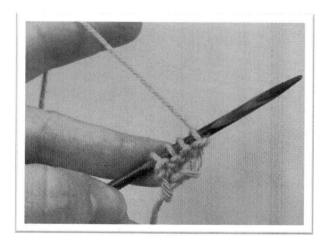

Step 3: Repeat Step 2.

Increases

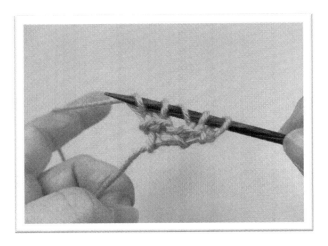

Step 4: Knit 2 stitches, Yarn Over (YO), Knit to the end of the row and turn the work.

Step 5: Repeat Step 4 until there are 20 stitches on the needle or until the dishcloth has reached the desired width.

Decreases

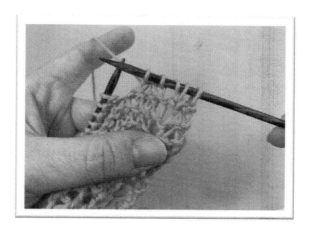

Step 6: Knit 1 stitch, Knit 2 Together (K2TOG), Yarn Over, Knit 1, K2TOG, Knit to the end of the row.

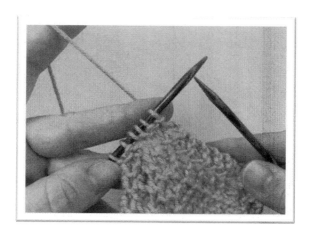

Step 7: Repeat Step 6 until 6 stitches remain on the needle.

Tip #20: For a variation on the dishcloth, use an SSK instead of a K2TOG and see if you can spot the difference in the result.

Bind Off

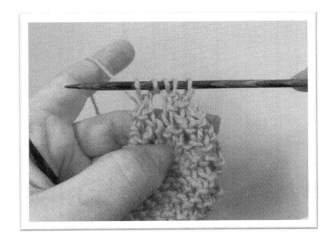

Step 8: Knit 1, K2TOG, Yarn Over, Knit 1, K2TOG. 5 stitches remaining.

Step 9: Knit 1, K2TOG, Yarn Over, K2TOG. 4 stitches remaining.

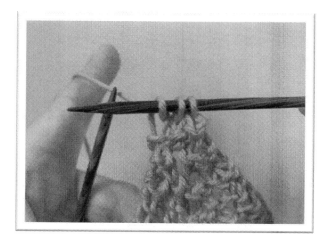

Step 10: Knit 1 stitch, K2TOG, Knit the last stitch. 3 stitches remaining.

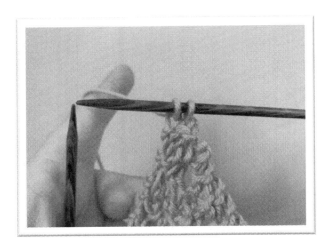

Step 11: K2TOG, Knit the last stitch. 2 stitches remaining.

Step 12: K2TOG then YO, pass the K2TOG over the YO and cut the working yarn. Pull the YO all the way through to make a knot. This is a simple Cinched Bind Off.

Tip #21: If you are feeling adventurous, you can use a crochet hook to chain stitches together and create a loop on the dishcloth to hang it up.

There are many variations that can be applied to this pattern, such as stripes, a different decrease (such as the SSK) or a different increase (the KFB), or even alternating knit rows and purl rows for stockinette stitch. Increasing to a wider point will yield a larger dishcloth and a narrower point will be a smaller one. If working swatches is not something a knitter prefers but they would still like to practice, dishcloths are excellent practice projects. One can never have too many dishcloths around and they make excellent handmade gifts as well. A set of three small matching dishcloths could be part of a facial gift set, or several coordinating larger ones for the kitchen. Knitters often modify patterns to meet their needs; dishcloths are a fantastic, low pressure way to test out new modification ideas.

Review (Abbreviated Pattern)

- CO 3 stitches with the Knitted Cast On
- (Knit 2, YO, Knit to end of row) repeat inside ( ) until desired width
- (Knit 2, YO, K2TOG, Knit to 4 stitches before the end, K2TOG, Knit 2) repeat inside ( ) until 6 stitches remain
- (Knit 2, YO, K2TOG) for two rows
- K2TOG, Knit 1 for one row
- K2TOG, YO, cut the yarn and pull the YO through

Chapter 7: Knitting a Scarf

Many, many, *many* first-time knitters start off with a scarf as their first project. There is absolutely nothing wrong with this! Other newbies may find the idea of a scarf as a first project daunting and they are not alone! The thought of knitting something the length of a scarf can be intimidating even for seasoned crafters. This is the reason that the dishcloth pattern precedes the scarf pattern in this book; by knitting a dishcloth, the newbie has all the experience they need to tackle a scarf. All the elements are there, just in a slightly different order. This pattern also incorporates a new element: stripes. Stripes are a simple and effective way to add interest to any project, whether they are subtle complementary colors or bold contrasting colors.

Tip #22: The first documented scarf wearer was Queen Nefertiti in 1350 BC.

The reason for the slipped stitch at the beginning of every row is to give the scarf a smooth, polished outside edge. If the knitter prefers to omit the slip stitch and knit across every row it will work just as well though the edge will have purl bumps.

Rainbow Scarf Supplies

Needles: US size 6, straight or circular

Yarn: Cascade 220 Worsted (alternate: Loops & Threads Impeccable Solids)

Amount: 400 yards total of red, yellow, green, blue, and violet colored yarns.

Optional: 200 yards (or less) of a dividing color and/or a stitch marker

Cast On

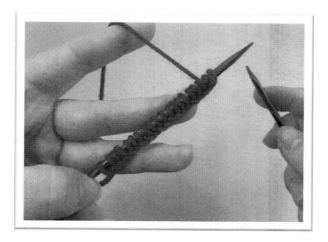

Step 1: Using the Knitted Cast On method described in Chapter 2 and the red yarn, cast on 20 stitches.

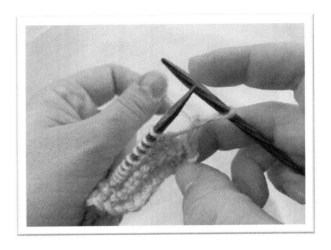

Step 1 **(Alternate)**: Cast On 20 stitches using the Dividing Color (DC).

Step 1.2 **(Optional)**: Slip 1 stitch purlwise then Knit across the row.

Step 1.3 **(Optional)**: Repeat Step 1.2 twice. There are now two purl ridges in the DC.

Step 1.4 **(Optional)**: Follow the instructions in Step A of the Changing Colors section to switch from the DC to the red yarn.

Knitting the Body

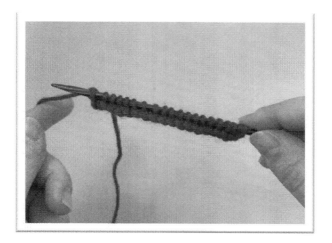

Step 2: Slip 1 stitch purlwise with the yarn in front, move the yarn to the back, then Knit across the row using the red yarn.

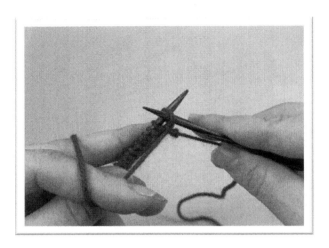

Step 3: Slip 1 stitch purlwise then Knit to the last stitch and Place Marker (PM) if using one.

Note: If knitting this pattern with different colors, when the Marker is on the right side of the work, that is the Right Side (RS). When the Marker is on the left side, that is the Wrong Side (WS). Changing colors will always begin on the Right Side. If knitting this pattern in one color, both the Right and Wrong Sides will appear the same.

Step 4: Repeat Step 2 until there are 30 purl ridges in red (58 more individual rows) ending after a WS row. Remember to slip the Marker if using one, do not knit it!

Step 4.1 (**DC option**): Follow the instructions in Step A of the Changing Colors section to switch from the red yarn to DC.

Step 4.2 (**DC option**): Slip 1 stitch purlwise and knit to the end of the row.

Step 4.3 (**DC option**): Repeat Step 4.2 three more times so there are 2 purl ridges in DC.

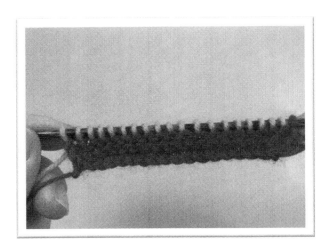

Step 5: Follow the instructions in Step A of the Changing Colors section to switch to the yellow yarn.

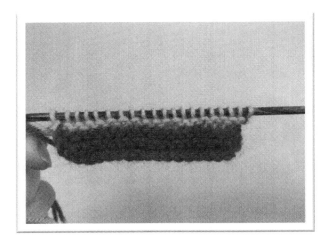

Step 6: Slip 1 stitch purlwise and knit to the end of the row.

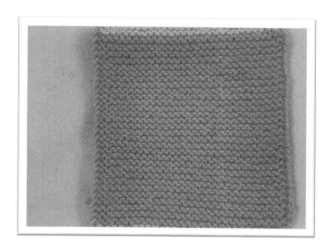

Step 7: Repeat Step 6 until there are 30 purl ridges in yellow (59 more individual rows) ending after a WS row.

Step 7.1 (**DC option**): Follow the instructions in Step A of the Changing Colors section to switch from the yellow yarn to DC.

Step 7.2 (**DC option**): Slip 1 stitch purlwise and knit to the end of the row.

Step 7.3 (**DC option**): Repeat Step 7.2 three more times so there are 2 purl ridges in DC.

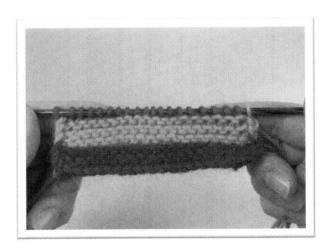

Step 8: Follow the instructions in Step A of the Changing Colors section to switch to the green yarn.

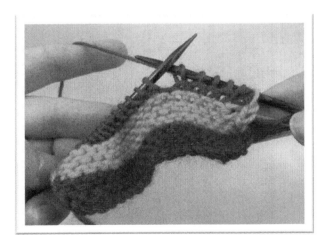

Step 9: Slip 1 stitch purlwise and knit to the end of the row.

Step 10: Repeat Step 9 until there are 30 purl ridges in green (59 more individual rows) ending after a WS row.

Step 10.1 (**DC option**): Follow the instructions in Step A of the Changing Colors section to switch from the green yarn to DC.

Step 10.2 (**DC option**): Slip 1 stitch purlwise and knit to the end of the row.

Step 10.3 (**DC option**): Repeat Step 10.2 three more times so there are 2 purl ridges in DC.

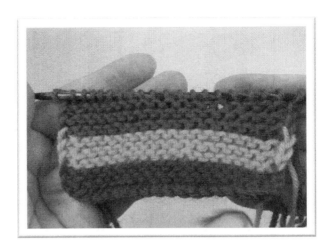

Step 11: Follow the instructions in Step A of the Changing Colors section to switch to the blue yarn.

Step 12: Slip 1 stitch purlwise and knit to the end of the row.

Step 13: Repeat Step 12 until there are 30 purl ridges in green (59 more individual rows) ending after a WS row.

> Step 13.1 (**DC option**): Follow the instructions in Step A of the Changing Colors section to switch from the blue yarn to DC.

> Step 13.2 (**DC option**): Slip 1 stitch purlwise and knit to the end of the row.

> Step 13.3 (**DC option**): Repeat Step 13.2 three more times so there are 2 purl ridges in DC.

Step 14: Follow the instructions in Step A of the Changing Colors section to switch to the violet yarn.

Step 15: Slip 1 stitch purlwise and knit to the end of the row.

Step 16: Repeat Step 15 until there are 30 purl ridges in violet (59 more individual rows) ending after a WS row.

Step 16.1 (**DC option**): Follow the instructions in Step A of the Changing Colors section to switch from the violet yarn to DC.

Step 16.2 (**DC option**): Slip 1 stitch purlwise and knit to the end of the row.

Step 16.3 (**DC option**): Repeat Step 16.2 three more times so there are 2 purl ridges in DC.

Step 17: Repeat Steps 1-16 to do the same color order again or reverse the color order and go from violet to blue to green to yellow to red.

Proceed to the Bind Off section when the scarf has reached the desired length.

Changing Colors

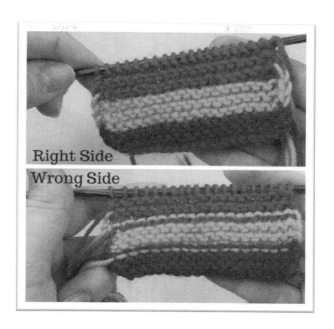

Right Side

Wrong Side

Step A: Beginning on a RS row, break or cut the previous color working yarn.

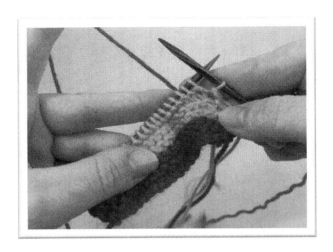

Step B: Secure the tail of the next color yarn, either around a finger or by tying it to the tail of the previous color yarn.

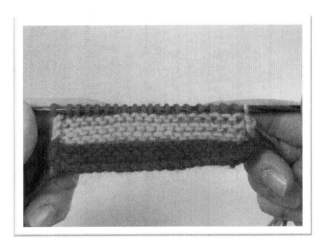

Step C: Tension the working yarn and knit one row then proceed to the next Step in the Body section.

Bind Off

Step 18: Follow the steps in the How to Bind Off section of Chapter 2 for the Knitted Bind Off.

Step 19: Using a tapestry needle, weave in any remaining tails.

Tip #23: Legend has it that the knitted scarf was first invented by the Third Duke of Kraków (Poland).

Scarves present a unique canvas for creativity given their long and (generally) narrow shape; stripes are just one of many options. There are patterns for lace scarves, double knit scarves, colorwork scarves, hooded scarves, scarves with pockets, skinny scarves, wide scarves, and so many more. There is little in the knitting world more satisfying than watching the length of a scarf grow as it is worked. A scarf is an enjoyable project for beginning and experienced knitters alike.

Review (Abbreviated Pattern)

- Cast On 20 stitches with the Knitted Cast On.
- Slip the first stitch of every row purlwise.
- Knit until there are 30 Purl ridges in each color (60 rows).
- Knit until each color appears twice (or desired length).
- Bind Off using the Knitted Bind Off.

Chapter 8: Knitting a Hat

Hats are another excellent early pattern choice for beginners, especially those who are interested in learning to knit in the round. Rows are called rounds when something is knit in a circular fashion with either Double Pointed Needles or a form of the Magic Loop Method. This hat pattern is very forgiving in terms of the fit, making it a great gift option as well. It will also utilize a different Cast On than the previous patterns, incorporate the purl stitch, and introduce a new Bind Off.

Tip #24: Knit hats are sometimes known as "Watch Caps" because they used to be worn while standing watch on a guard post or ship.

Cat Ear Hat Supplies

Needles: US size 6, circular or DPN

Yarn: Cascade 220 Worsted (alternate: Loops & Threads Impeccable Solids)

Amount: 200 yards or less

Notions: Stitch markers

Cast On

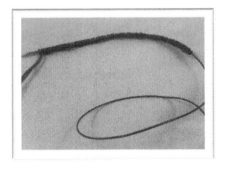

Step 1: Using the Long Tail Cast On method, mentioned in Chapter 2, Cast On 72 stitches (or whatever number of stitches fits comfortably around the head of the intended wearer).

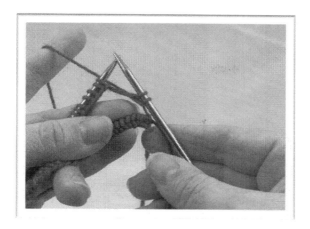

Step 2: Join in the round using either the Magic/Traveling Loop Method or Double Pointed Needles and knit one round.

Knitting the Brim

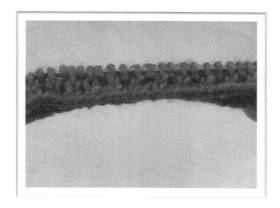

Step 3: (Knit 1, Purl 1) repeat inside ( ) until the end of the round.

Step 4: Repeat Step 3 nine times.

Knitting the Body

Step 5: Knit until the end of the round.

Step 6: Repeat Step 5 until the hat measures about 8 inches or can easily be held closed on the head of the recipient.

Finishing

Step 7: Using the Three Needle Bind Off method, mentioned in Chapter 2, bind off the stitches, cut the yarn, then weave in any remaining ends.

Tip #25: Sailors used to add pompoms to their Watch Caps because it gave them extra protection against bumping their heads in rough weather.

Hats are like the dishcloth of knitting in the round for new knitters; they can provide opportunity for new skills and are satisfyingly fast to make. Gauge is not as crucial for hats as it is with other garments or accessories, and hats knit up quickly with worsted weight yarns or heavier. The hat pattern covered in this chapter is one of a few that does not include crown decreases or increases. Generally, hat construction includes a brim, body, and a crown with increases or decreases depending on which direction it is knit from (top down or brim up). It can be difficult, especially for a beginner, to estimate where to start/end the crown of the hat and still have the desired finished length. For that reason, this chapter covers a pattern where the knitter can work the hat until it is the desired length then immediately bind off for a perfect fit.

Review (Abbreviated Pattern)

- Cast on 72 stitches (or desired amount) using the Long Tail Cast On.
- Join in the round and (Knit 1, Purl 1) repeating inside the ( ) for ten rounds.
- Knit until the hat measures 8 inches or the desired length.
- Use the Three Needle Bind Off and weave any ends.

Chapter 9: Knitting Fingerless Gloves

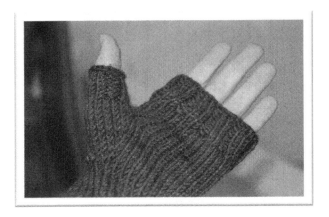

When it comes to keeping hands warm and knitting up quickly, fingerless gloves are hard to beat. Double Pointed Needles may be necessary to comfortably knit small tubes for the thumbs, however it is still possible to use the Magic Loop method. The truly ambitious knitters will go for full fingered gloves, however, that can be a tedious and methodic project for a beginner. The pattern included in this chapter forgoes the fingers and focuses on fascinating cables.

Tip #26: Abby Condon, an early US female entrepreneur, secured herself a contract to knit mittens for Civil War soldiers. Her group's mittens cost the Army 25 cents a pair.

Fingerless Glove Supplies

Needles: US size 6, circular or DPN

Yarn: Cascade 220 Worsted (alternate: Loops &
Threads Impeccable Solids)

Amount: 200 yards or less

Notions: Stitch markers, tapestry needle, cable needle
or extra needle (such as a DPN), and waste yarn

Cast On

Step 1: Cast on 36 stitches using the Knitted Cast On
method.

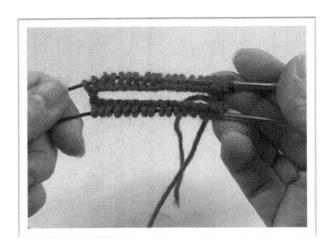

Step 2: Being careful not to twist the cast on edge, join in the round and place a stitch marker (optional).

Step 3: (Knit 2, Purl 2) all the way around.

Step 4: Repeat Step 3 nine times.

Knitting the Body

Step 5: Knit across one round.

Beginning of Cable Pattern

Step 6: Knit 3, Purl 2, Knit 8, Purl 2, Knit to end of round.

Step 7: Repeat Step 6 three times.

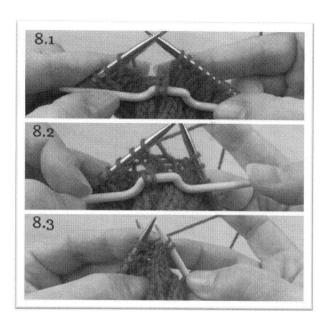

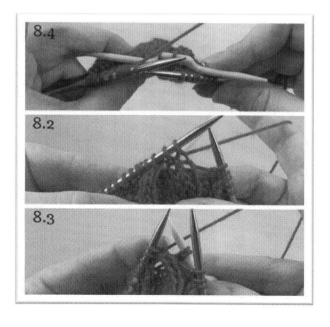

Step 8: Knit 3, Purl 2, slip 2 stitches onto cable needle and hold in front of work[8.1], Knit 2 stitches from the left needle[8.2], place the 2 slipped stitches back onto the left needle and knit them[8.3], slip the next 2 stitches onto cable needle and hold in back of work[8.4], Knit 2 stitches from the left needle[8.5], place the 2 slipped stitches back onto the left needle and knit them[8.6], Purl 2, Knit to end of round.

> Step 8 Abbreviated: K3, P2, Slip 2 onto cable needle front, K2, K2 from cable needle, Slip 2 onto cable needle back, K2, K2 from cable needle, P2, K to end of round.

Step 9: Knit 3, Purl 2, Knit 8, Purl 2, Knit to end of round.

End of Cable Pattern

Step 10: Repeat Cable Pattern steps four times and move onto the thumb gusset instructions for the appropriate hand.

Working the Thumb Gusset

Left Hand

Step 11: Knit 3, Purl 2, Knit 8, Purl 2, **Knit to 4 stitches before the end of round.**

Step 12: Place a stitch marker, Knit Front and Back (KFB), Knit 1, Knit Front and Back again, place another stitch marker, **Knit 2**. End of round. (5 stitches between markers)

Step 13: Knit 3, Purl 2, Knit 8, Purl 2, Knit to first thumb marker, Slip Marker (SM), Knit to second thumb marker, Slip Marker, **Knit 2**.

Step 14: Knit 3, Purl 2, Knit 8, Purl 2, Knit to first thumb marker, Slip Marker (SM), Knit Front and Back (KFB), Knit to one stitch before the second thumb marker, Knit Front and Back, Slip Marker, **Knit 2**. (7 stitches between markers)

Step 15: Knit 3, Purl 2, (slip 2 stitches onto cable needle and hold in front of work, Knit 2 stitches from the left needle, place the 2 slipped stitches back onto the left needle and knit them, slip the next 2 stitches onto cable needle and hold in back of work, Knit 2 stitches from the left needle, place the 2 slipped stitches back onto the left needle and knit them)[8.1-8.6], Purl 2, Knit to the first thumb marker, Slip Marker, Knit to second marker, Slip Marker, **Knit 2**.

Step 15 Abbreviated: K3, P2, Slip 2 onto cable needle front, K2, K2 from cable needle, Slip 2 onto cable needle back, K2, K2 from cable needle, P2, K first thumb marker, SM, knit to second marker, SM, **K2**.

Step 16: Knit 3, Purl 2, Knit 8, Purl 2, Knit to first thumb marker, Slip Marker (SM), Knit Front and Back (KFB), Knit to one stitch before the second thumb marker, Knit Front and Back, Slip Marker, **Knit 2**. (9 stitches between markers)

Step 17: Knit 3, Purl 2, Knit 8, Purl 2, Knit to first thumb marker, Slip Marker (SM), Knit to second thumb marker, Slip Marker, **Knit 2**.

Step 18: Knit 3, Purl 2, Knit 8, Purl 2, Knit to first thumb marker, Slip Marker (SM), Knit Front and Back (KFB), Knit to one stitch before the second thumb

marker, Knit Front and Back, Slip Marker, **Knit 2**. (11 stitches between markers)

Step 19: Knit 3, Purl 2, Knit 8, Purl 2, Knit to first thumb marker, Slip Marker (SM), Knit to second thumb marker, Slip Marker, **Knit 2**.

Step 20: Knit 3, Purl 2, (slip 2 stitches onto cable needle and hold in front of work, Knit 2 stitches from the left needle, place the 2 slipped stitches back onto the left needle and knit them, slip the next 2 stitches onto cable needle and hold in back of work, Knit 2 stitches from the left needle, place the 2 slipped stitches back onto the left needle and knit them)[8.1-8.6], Purl 2, Knit to the first thumb marker, Slip Marker, Knit to second marker, Knit Front and Back (KFB), Knit to one stitch before the second thumb marker, Knit Front and Back, Slip Marker, **Knit 2**. (13 stitches between markers)

> Step 20 Abbreviated: K3, P2, Slip 2 onto cable needle front, K2, K2 from cable needle, Slip 2 onto cable needle back, K2, K2 from cable needle, P2, K first thumb marker, SM, KFB, knit to second marker, KFB, SM, **K2**. (13 stitches between markers)

Step 21: Knit 3, Purl 2, Knit 8, Purl 2, Knit to first thumb marker, Slip Marker (SM), Knit to second thumb marker, Slip Marker, **Knit 2**.

Step 22: Knit 3, Purl 2, Knit 8, Purl 2, Knit to first thumb marker, Slip Marker (SM), Knit Front and Back (KFB), Knit to one stitch before the second thumb marker, Knit Front and Back, Slip Marker, **Knit 2**. (15 stitches between markers)

Step 23: Knit 3, Purl 2, Knit 8, Purl 2, Knit to first thumb marker, use the tapestry needle and thread the stitches between the markers onto the waste yarn, cast on 3 stitches using the Backwards Loop method, **Knit 2**. Thumb gusset stitch markers are no longer needed.

Step 24: Knit 3, Purl 2, Knit 8, Purl 2, Knit to end of round.

Step 25: Knit 3, Purl 2, (slip 2 stitches onto cable needle and hold in front of work, Knit 2 stitches from the left needle, place the 2 slipped stitches back onto the left needle and knit them, slip the next 2 stitches onto cable needle and hold in back of work, Knit 2 stitches from the left needle, place the 2 slipped stitches back onto the left needle and knit them)$^{8.1-8.6}$, Purl 2, Knit to end of round.

Step 25 Abbreviated: K3, P2, Slip 2 onto cable needle front, K2, K2 from cable needle, Slip 2 onto cable needle back, K2, K2 from cable needle, P2, K to end of round.

Step 26: Knit 3, Purl 2, Knit 8, Purl 2, Knit to end of round.

Step 27: Repeat Step 26 twice then move onto the Knitting the Cuff section.

Right Hand

Step 11: Knit 3, Purl 2, Knit 8, Purl 2, **Knit 5 then move on to Step 12.**

Step 12: Place a stitch marker, Knit Front and Back (KFB), Knit 1, Knit Front and Back again, place another stitch marker, **Knit to end of round.** (5 stitches between markers)

Step 13: Knit 3, Purl 2, Knit 8, Purl 2, Knit to first thumb marker, Slip Marker (SM), Knit to second thumb marker, Slip Marker, **Knit to end of round**.

Step 14: Knit 3, Purl 2, Knit 8, Purl 2, Knit to first thumb marker, Slip Marker (SM), Knit Front and Back (KFB), Knit to one stitch before second thumb marker, Knit Front and Back, Slip Marker, **Knit to end of round**. (7 stitches between markers)

Step 15: Knit 3, Purl 2, (slip 2 stitches onto cable needle and hold in front of work, Knit 2 stitches from the left needle, place the 2 slipped stitches back onto the left needle and knit them, slip the next 2 stitches onto cable needle and hold in back of work, Knit 2 stitches from the left needle, place the 2 slipped stitches back onto the left needle and knit them)[8.1-8.6], Purl 2, Knit to the first thumb marker, Slip Marker, Knit to second marker, Slip Marker, **Knit to end of round**.

Step 15 Abbreviated: K3, P2, Slip 2 onto cable needle front, K2, K2 from cable needle, Slip 2 onto cable needle back, K2, K2 from cable needle, P2, K first thumb marker, SM, knit to second marker, SM, **Knit to end of round**.

Step 16: Knit 3, Purl 2, Knit 8, Purl 2, Knit to first thumb marker, Slip Marker (SM), Knit Front and Back (KFB), Knit to one stitch before the second thumb marker, Knit Front and Back, Slip Marker, **Knit to end of round**. (9 stitches between markers)

Step 17: Knit 3, Purl 2, Knit 8, Purl 2, Knit to first thumb marker, Slip Marker (SM), Knit to second thumb marker, Slip Marker, **Knit to end of round**.

Step 18: Knit 3, Purl 2, Knit 8, Purl 2, Knit to first thumb marker, Slip Marker (SM), Knit Front and Back (KFB), Knit to one stitch before the second thumb marker, Knit Front and Back, Slip Marker, **Knit to end of round**. (11 stitches between markers)

Step 19: Knit 3, Purl 2, Knit 8, Purl 2, Knit to first thumb marker, Slip Marker (SM), Knit to second thumb marker, Slip Marker, **Knit to end of round**.

Step 20: Knit 3, Purl 2, (slip 2 stitches onto cable needle and hold in front of work, Knit 2 stitches from the left needle, place the 2 slipped stitches back onto the left

needle and knit them, slip the next 2 stitches onto cable needle and hold in back of work, Knit 2 stitches from the left needle, place the 2 slipped stitches back onto the left needle and knit them)[8.1-8.6], Purl 2, Knit to the first thumb marker, Slip Marker, Knit to second marker, Knit Front and Back (KFB), Knit to one stitch before the second thumb marker, Knit Front and Back, Slip Marker, **Knit to end of round**. (13 stitches between markers)

> Step 20 Abbreviated: K3, P2, Slip 2 onto cable needle front, K2, K2 from cable needle, Slip 2 onto cable needle back, K2, K2 from cable needle, P2, K first thumb marker, SM, KFB, knit to second marker, KFB, SM, **Knit to end of round**. (13 stitches between markers)

Step 21: Knit 3, Purl 2, Knit 8, Purl 2, Knit to first thumb marker, Slip Marker (SM), Knit to second thumb marker, Slip Marker, **Knit to end of round**.

Step 22: Knit 3, Purl 2, Knit 8, Purl 2, Knit to first thumb marker, Slip Marker (SM), Knit Front and Back (KFB), Knit to one stitch before the second thumb marker, Knit Front and Back, Slip Marker, **Knit to end of round**. (15 stitches between markers)

Step 23: Knit 3, Purl 2, Knit 8, Purl 2, Knit to first thumb marker, use the tapestry needle and thread the stitches between the markers onto the waste yarn, cast on 3 stitches using the Backwards Loop method, **Knit to end of round**. Thumb gusset stitch markers are no longer needed.

Step 24: Knit 3, Purl 2, Knit 8, Purl 2, Knit to end of round.

Step 25: Knit 3, Purl 2, (slip 2 stitches onto cable needle and hold in front of work, Knit 2 stitches from the left needle, place the 2 slipped stitches back onto the left needle and knit them, slip the next 2 stitches onto cable needle and hold in back of work, Knit 2 stitches from the left needle, place the 2 slipped stitches back onto the left needle and knit them)$^{8.1-8.6}$, Purl 2, Knit to end of round.

> Step 23 Abbreviated: K3, P2, Slip 2 onto cable needle front, K2, K2 from cable needle, Slip 2 onto cable needle back, K2, K2 from cable needle, P2, K to end of round.

Step 26: Knit 3, Purl 2, Knit 8, Purl 2, Knit to end of round.

Step 27: Repeat Step 26 twice then move onto the Knitting the Cuff section.

Knitting the Cuff

Step 28: (Knit 2, Purl 2) all the way around.

Step 29: Repeat Step 28 nine times.

Bind Off and Thumb

Step 30: Bind off using Jeny's Surprisingly Stretchy Bind Off method.

Step 31: Place the 15 thumb stitches onto a circular needle (or needles if using DPNs) and remove waste yarn.

Step 32: Pick up and knit 1 stitch in the cast on stitches.

Step 33: Continue knitting the 15 thumb stitches, place marker (optional) then join in the round.

Step 34: (Knit 2, Purl 2) all the way around.

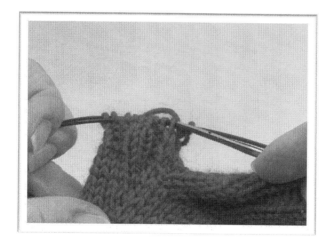

Step 35: Repeat Step 34 four times.

Step 36: Bind off the thumb using the Knitted Bind Off method.

Tip #27: Condon recruited 1500 women to knit for her Army contract, and in one year they produced 15,000 dozen mittens.

If longer gloves are desired, work additional cable repeats prior to beginning the thumb gusset. To allow better fit for larger hands, increase the Cast On number of stitches in increments of 12, which spreads out over the gloves to +6 on the front and +6 on the back. When adding additional stitches, the sets of +6 being added to the front should also be split in half so that there are +3 stitches per new set of 12 on either side of the cable pattern. For example, if 48 stitches have been cast on, the first cable round would look something like this:

Knit 6, Purl 2, Knit 8, Purl 2, Knit to end of round.

Alternatively, if multiple sets of cables are desired, the same cable pattern can be repeated, rather than adding stitches to either side. Each set of cables is 12 stitches, to have two sets of cables on the front of the gloves, cast on a minimum of 60 stitches. The placement of the thumb gussets can be adjusted as well by shifting the beginning of the gusset right or left on the back of the gloves. To move the left thumb gusset inward, markers could be placed 5 stitches before the end of round, rather than 3. Likewise, shifting the right thumb gusset inward can be marked at 7 stitches after the last cable Purl, instead of 5. Swatching is an excellent way of determining what changes may need to be made, if any.

Review (Abbreviated Pattern)

- Cast on 36 stitches using the Long Tail Cast On method.
- Join in the round and knit 10 rounds of (K2, P2) ribbing.
- Cable Pattern:

- (K3, P2, K8, P2, K to end of round)x3
- K3, P2, Slip 2 onto cable needle front, K2, K2 from cable needle, Slip 2 onto cable needle back, K2, K2 from cable needle, P2, K to end of round.
- K3, P2, K8, P2, K to end of round

- <u>End of Cable Pattern</u> (Repeat x4)
- Left Thumb Gusset (Continue following Cable Pattern):
  - Thumb Row 1: (Cable Pattern), **K to 3 stitches before the end of round,** PM, M1, K1, M1, PM, K2
  - Thumb Row 2: (Cable Pattern), K to end of Round
  - Thumb Row 3: (Cable Pattern), K to Marker, SM, M1, K to Marker, M1, SM, K2
  - Continuing the Cable Pattern, repeat Thumb Rows 2-3 until there are 13 stitches between the markers.
  - Final Thumb Row: (Cable Pattern), K to Marker and remove, thread the 13 thumb stitches onto waste yarn with a tapestry needle, remove the second Marker, and cast on 3 stitches using the Backwards Loop method.
  - (K3, P2, K8, P2, K to end of round)x2
  - Move on to Cuff Section
- Right Thumb Gusset (Continue following Cable Pattern):
  - Thumb Row 1: (Cable Pattern), **K to 3 stitches before the end of round,** PM, M1, K1, M1, PM, K2
  - Thumb Row 2: (Cable Pattern), K to end of Round
  - Thumb Row 3: (Cable Pattern), K to Marker, SM, M1, K to Marker, M1, SM, K2

- Continuing the Cable Pattern, repeat Thumb Rows 2-3 until there are 13 stitches between the markers.
- Final Thumb Row: (Cable Pattern), K to Marker and remove, thread the 13 thumb stitches onto waste yarn with a tapestry needle, remove the second Marker, and cast on 3 stitches using the Backwards Loop method.
- (K3, P2, K8, P2, K to end of round)x2
- Move on to Cuff Section.

- (K2, P2) all the way around, repeat () x 9
- BO using JSSBO.
- Put the 13 thumb stitches back onto the needles and pick up 3 of the CO stitches, join in the round.
- (K2, P2) all the way around, repeat () x 4
- BO using Knitted BO.

Chapter 10: Knitting a Cowl

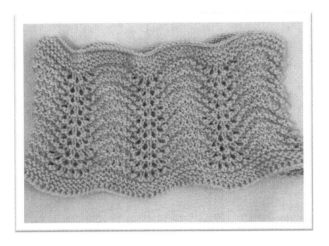

A cowl is like a scarf in function but different in construction. Often, cowls are knit in the round, some are worked in a mobius loop (also known as an infinity scarf). Some cowls can be long, able to be wrapped twice around the wearer's neck while others are short and cling close to the skin. Cowls can be stylish and functional, keeping the cool breezes at bay while still looking smart. Worn alone or tucked into a jacket, these are the perfect accessories for the changing seasons.

Tip #28: The term cowl originally refers to a large, loose hooded cloak worn mainly by monks in the 10th and 11th centuries.

Cowl Supplies

Needles: US size 6, circular or DPN

Yarn: Cascade 220 Worsted (alternate: Loops &
Threads Impeccable Solids)

Amount: 200 yards

Notions: Stitch markers, tapestry needle

Cast On

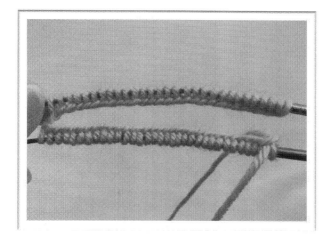

Step 1: Cast on 126 stitches using the Long Tail Cast On.

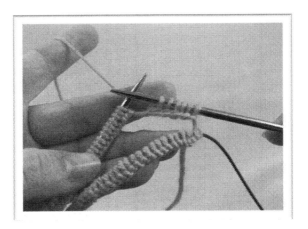

Step 2: Being careful not to twist the cast on edge, join in the round, place a beginning of the round marker (optional), and knit two rounds.

> Note: the cast on edge may be a little tight during the first round, however, it will relax after it is knitted.

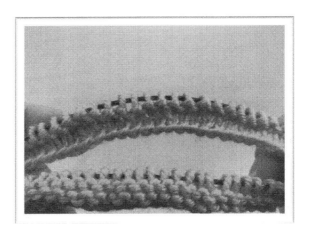

Step 3: Purl one round.

Step 4: Knit one round.

Step 5: Repeat Steps 3-4 twice.

Knitting the Body

Note: This section of the cowl is provided in both written instructions as well as a chart. Knitters may compare the written portion to the charted portion to see how they correspond. Whether using written, charted, or both, this lace section will be worked a total of 10 times.

Written Pattern

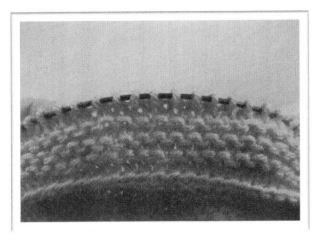

Step 6: Knit 2 rounds

Step 7: Slip Slip Knit 3 times, (Yarn Over, Knit) 6 times, Slip Slip Knit 3 times. Repeat these 18 stitches all the way around. If helpful, place additional stitch markers between repeats to make them easier to distinguish.

Step 8: Purl 1 round.

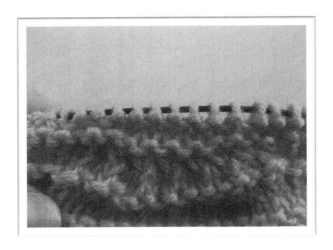

Step 9: Repeat Steps 6-8 nine more times then move on to the Bind Off section.

Charted Pattern

Step 6: Beginning in Column 1, Row 1, follow this chart and repeat these 18 stitches all the way around.

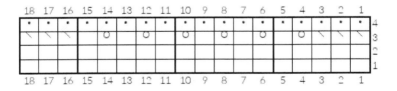

Created on **chart-minder.com**

Stitch Key

	Knit (K)		Yarn Over (YO)
	Purl (P)		Slip Slip Knit (SSK)

Step 7: Repeat the chart rounds (1 through 4) 9 more times then move on to the Bind Off section.

Bind Off

Step 8: Purl 1 round.

Step 9: Knit 1 round.

Step 10: Repeat Steps 8-9 twice and bind off using Jeny's Surprisingly Stretchy Bind Off

Tip #29: Cowl neckline garments were created by Madeleine Vionnet in the 1920's though cowl neck sweaters did not become popular until the 1970's.

This cowl can be adjusted lengthwise by working additional 4-round repeats; for a shorter cowl, work fewer repeats and for a taller one work more. To adjust widthwise, add or subtract stitches in multiples of 18; for a larger loop cast on 144 or 162 and for a smaller loop cast on 108 or 90. Old Shale is the name of the lace pattern used within the cowl, it is a classic Shetland pattern originating from the Shetland islands of Scotland.

Review (Abbreviated Pattern)

- Using the Long Tail Cast On, cast on 126 stitches.

- Being careful not to twist, place a marker, join in the round, and knit 2 rounds.
- (Purl 1 round, Knit 1 round) three times.
- Lace Pattern:
    - Knit 2 rounds
    - *SSKx3, (YO, K)x3, SSKx3; rep from * all the way around
    - Purl 1 round
- Work the Lace Pattern ten times.
- (Purl 1 round, Knit 1 round) three times.
- Bind off using Jeny's Surprisingly Stretchy Bind Off.

Chapter 11: How to Troubleshoot and Fix Common Knitting Mistakes

The first step in correcting an issue is recognizing that there is a problem. The second step is determining specifically what that problem is and then moving on towards a solution. One thing that new knitters come across is that they are aware there is a mistake in their work, however, they may not be confident enough in their troubleshooting skills to determine the solution. This chapter covers some of the most common knitting errors that a beginner may come across. Although, this is not comprehensive and there are many more mistakes to be made and fixed. If a new knitter is unable to diagnose their own issue, it is recommended to reach out to another, more experienced knitter, for additional guidance. Video calls can be a valuable resource if the experienced knitter is not available in person.

Tip #30: Before working a potentially difficult section of knitting, add a "Lifeline" by threading waste yarn through a tapestry needle and weaving it through the stitches in the previous row. The Lifeline allows you to rip back to that point without dropping stitches past it.

Learning to Read the Stitches

Swatching is mentioned many times throughout this book and this chapter will be no exception. In addition to the benefits already illustrated for working a swatch before beginning a project, another reason is that it gives the knitter an idea of how their stitches will "read". This means that the knitter will know what their stitches are supposed to look like and, therefore, what they are not supposed to look like. If the pattern is calling for a right slanted decrease, but the knitter's K2TOG is leaning left in the swatch, they may need to re-visit how to execute a K2TOG so that it leans the correct direction. A swatch will provide real-time feedback on the knitter's gauge as well as the specific stitches worked. A looser gauge SSK will look different than one knit with a tighter gauge.

There are characteristics that will apply to all knitters, in most cases. Identifying the problem is necessary before attempting a solution, especially for those who are learning a new skill. One notion that will come in particularly handy when fixing common knitting mistakes is the crochet hook. It is adept at bringing up dropped stitches, or simply holding stitches to the side while their counterparts are being fixed.

Tip #31: "Rip it" or "rip back" refers to pulling out rows one at a time to go back to a previous row in a pattern with the intent of correcting an issue.

Knit Stitch Characteristics

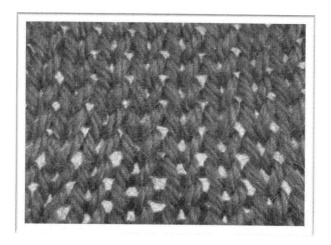

The Knit stitch has an unmistakable V-shape to the legs once it has been worked. One method of counting rows, especially in Stockinette stitch, is to count the V's in a column. The other main characteristic with the Knit stitch is that the Purl bump is located behind it on what is typically the wrong side of the work.

Purl Stitch Characteristics

The Purl stitch is the opposite of the Knit stitch in
nearly every way. There is a V-shape to the legs of the
Purl stitch, like the Knit stitch, however it is located on
the back of the work. The Purl bump is located on the
front of the work, which is the origin of the name "Purl
bump". Purl bumps are sometimes more difficult to
count than the V's of Knit stitches when it comes to
counting rows. Garter ridges, for example, are
considered 2 rows per ridge, whereas in something such
as Reverse Stockinette the fabric consists entirely of
Purl bumps and each bump is a single row.

Yarn Over Characteristics

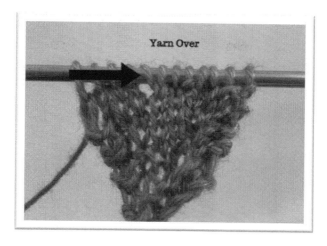

There are two distinct features of the Yarn Over that separates it from other increases. The first is the large hole it leaves in the fabric because a new stitch "column" is being added without the use of any other stitches. The second feature of the Yarn Over is the lack of a Purl bump. The Yarn Over is not working an existing stitch, therefore there is no bump to shift to the back or front such as with Knits and Purls. Yarn Overs are often key components of lace patterns for this and many other reasons.

M1L and M1R Characteristics

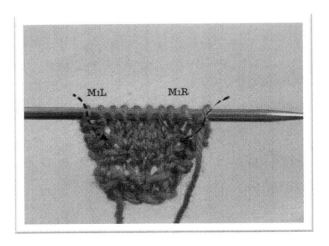

Unlike the Yarn Over that creates a stitch with the working yarn, the Make 1 Left (M1L) and Make 1 Right (M1R) increases use existing stitch structures—specifically the bar between two stitches—to create a new stitch. In the same way that K2TOG and SSK decreases lean to the right and left, the stitches created by M1L and M1R lean as well. As their name implies, Make 1 Left is a left leaning increase and Make 1 Right is a right leaning increase. M1L and M1R are distinguished from K2TOG and SSK by looking at the base of the stitch. The decreases will consist of one stitch overlapping another, the increases will consist of a new stitch "coming out" of a smaller stitch.

KFB Characteristics

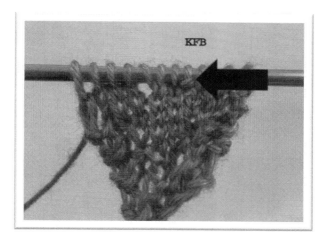

The Knit Front and Back (KFB) increase utilizes an existing stitch by working it twice, knitting the front leg then the back leg. This results in two Purl bumps, rather than one, on each side of the fabric. A KFB increase is nearly invisible in Garter Stitch due to the double Purl Bumps and because it does not lean one way or the other.

K2TOG and SSK Characteristics

Commonly found in the toes of socks, the Knit 2 Together (K2TOG) and Slip Slip Knit (SSK) decreases are a Knitter's best friend. Leaning decreases can give directionality and texture to a fabric to make it visually interesting. Both the K2TOG and SSK decreases will overlap with a stitch next to them, combining two stitches into one. The K2TOG will overlap the stitch to its immediate right, which is what causes it to lean to the right. Whereas the SSK will overlap the stitch to its left, giving it the left lean. Which stitch overlaps a specific direction has to do with its place on the left needle before moving to the right needle. In a K2TOG, the right needle enters the second stitch on the left needle before it enters the first stitch, whereas in an SSK the right needle enters the first stitch then the second. While reading stitches, if a knitter is unsure whether they are looking at a K2TOG or SSK, they should examine which of the overlapping stitches is on top and the direction it is leaning.

Fixing Dropped Stitches

One of the early mistakes that new knitters can make is dropping a stitch. This happens when a live stitch, which is a stitch that has not been bound off, comes loose from the needle holding it and starts to fall down the rows. All knitters have done this at some point in their crafting career; it happens to everyone. Learning to fix dropped stitches in a variety of scenarios will setup a beginning knitter for success. The alternative to fixing dropped stitches is to rip out all the worked rows down to where the stitch stopped falling, potentially resulting in several hours of lost work. Dropped stitches are a good reason for knitters to have at least one crochet hook in their craft stash, though they are not a necessity.

Dropped Knit Stitches

One clue that a dropped knit stitch has occurred is the appearance of a "ladder" between two stitches that starts off wide and narrows the further down it goes. At the bottom-most point of this ladder will be a loose loop of a stitch that will continue to fall until it is stopped, either by a needle or until it reaches the project edge. It is crucial in fixing this issue that no additional tension is placed on the fabric until the stitch has been secured in some way. A tapestry needle, cable needle, or even a safety pin will hold the errant stitch in place.

Step 1: Secure the loose stitch to keep it from dropping any further.

Step 2: Identify the bars between the stitches in the rows above the dropped stitch; they will look like rungs on a ladder. The bar immediately above the dropped stitch should correspond to the next row after the row where the stitch landed.

Step 3: Using a crochet hook or knitting needles, pull the bar above through the dropped stitch from back to front (crochet hook) or lift the dropped stitch over the bar from left to right (knitting needles).

Step 4: Repeat Step 3 until the dropped stitch has been brought up and aligns with the other live stitches on the knitting needles.

Dropped Purl Stitches

If a beginning knitter can correct a dropped Knit stitch, then fixing a dropped Purl stitch should seem familiar. The bars between stitches will appear looking like the rungs of a ladder. However, unlike the dropped Knit stitch which fell in front of the bars, a dropped Purl stitch will fall behind the bars. This can make the dropped stitch more difficult to locate without causing them to fall further.

Step 1: Secure the loose stitch to keep it from dropping any further.

Step 2: Identify the bars between the stitches in the rows above the dropped stitch, they will look like rungs on a ladder. The bar immediately above the dropped stitch should correspond to the next row after the row where the stitch landed.

Step 3: Using a crochet hook or knitting needles, pull the bar above through the dropped stitch from front to back (crochet hook) or lift the dropped stitch over the bar from right to left (knitting needles).

Step 4: Repeat Step 3 until the dropped stitch has been brought up and aligns with the other live stitches on the knitting needles.

Dropped Decreases

Decreases can be tricky stitches, especially to identify if they have been dropped. Often, they will look like more than one stitch has been dropped because the overlapped stitches may start to fall independently of each other. To determine whether multiple dropped stitches are the result of a dropped decrease or if there truly should be more than one, the knitter should compare the row the stitch(es) fell from against the pattern as well as their stitch count. If, including the dropped stitch(es), the knitter has the correct number of total stitches then it was not a decrease that was dropped. However, if the knitter has more stitches than needed this likely confirms that a decrease was dropped. Finally, if the knitter is no longer able to locate the decrease in the fabric where the pattern specifies it, the stitchers should be corrected as a decrease.

Step 1: Secure the loose stitch to keep it from dropping any further.

Step 2: Identify the bars between the stitches in the rows above the dropped stitches and determine which row should contain the decrease. It is possible that the individual stitches fell past the row where they were decreased.

Step 3: Using the steps from the Dropped Knit/Purl Stitch section as necessary, bring the dropped stitches up to the decrease row.

Step 3: Using a crochet hook or knitting needles, pull the bar above through both the dropped stitches from front to back (crochet hook) or lift both the dropped stitches over the bar from right to left (knitting needles).

Step 4: Repeat Step 2-3 as necessary until the dropped stitch has been brought up and aligns with the other live stitches on the knitting needles. The total stitch count should now be correct.

Dropped or Forgotten Increases

Increases that have been dropped (or forgotten) are some of the easiest to fix if they are caught early. Many times, the knitter can quickly work a forgotten increase stitch into a previous row using the bar between the stitches. A leaning increase will require the knitter utilize the bars from two previous rows, not just the row immediately prior to the current one.

Yarn Over: If the YO was not worked before it was dropped, simply pick up the bar between the stitches where the YO should be, Knit or Purl the YO as specified in the pattern, and continue the row normally. If the YO was worked before it was dropped, locate the first "rung" of the ladder and use that as the dropped stitch. Follow the steps from the Dropped Knit/Purl Stitch section as necessary.

M1L: Lift the bar between stitches immediately below where the M1L should be as well as the bar below that one. Following the steps from the Dropped Knit Stitch section as necessary, twist the bottom bar on the left needle so it looks like the legs are crossed, then pull the top bar through the bottom bar or loop the bottom over the top.

M1R: Lift the bar between stitches immediately below where the M1L should be as well as the bar below that one. Following the steps from the Dropped Knit Stitch section as necessary, pull the top bar through the bottom bar or loop the bottom over the top. This will not lean as written, if a lean is desired the stitch can be twisted before being worked to give the appearance that it is leaning.

KFB: It is not advisable to "pick up" a forgotten KFB as it will make the surrounding stitches too tight and they will not look as the designer intended. Dropped KFB increases can be corrected in the same way that a M1R stitch is corrected by pulling the top of two bars through the bottom.

Fixing Too Many Stitches

Common Scenarios:

"My knitting isn't straight"

"My knitting is getting longer"

"My knitting has a slanted edge"

If a knitter finds themselves in one of the above scenarios, chances are high the issues are due to having too many stitches. Edges will start to angle outwards, there may be obviously less room on the needles to fit the stitches, or the knitter has reached the end of a repeat and found leftover stitches. There are a couple of solutions available, depending on where and why the extra stitches occurred.

Tip #32: Knitters sometimes jokingly refer to mistakes they leave in as "design features" or "bonus features".

<u>The mistake has been made repeatedly over several rows</u>. First, the knitter needs to establish where the accidental increase is happening while they work. Then the knitter should decide if the extra length or width caused by the extra stitches is acceptable to keep or if they prefer to correct it. Should the knitter wish to correct the error, the simplest way to do this is to rip back to before the error started once the accidental increase has been located.

<u>There are extra stitches at the end of a repeat.</u> This could be due to a missed decrease or an extra increase from the previous row. The knitter should carefully compare the repeat to the pattern to ensure no stitches were missed, then analyze the previous row(s) in the same way until the issue is found. Once the error has been located, the knitter can choose to either add decreases at the end of the repeat to fix the stitch count or go back to the source of the error and correct it there.

It may be necessary to rip back to the problem or perhaps it can be fixed by dropping a stitch or two down then working them up the correct way (as described in the previous the Fixing Dropped Stitches section).

Fixing Too Few Stitches

Common Scenarios:

"I don't have enough stitches at the end of the round to complete the pattern"

"I'm missing a stitch (or more) at the end of a pattern repeat"

"My knitting is getting narrower"

Although having too few stitches may seem like a different issue than having too many, it can occur under similar circumstances. Edges of the knitting may start to slant inwards or there will not be enough stitches to complete a repeat. As with having too many stitches, having too few stitches will have multiple solutions based on the scenario.

<u>The mistake has been made repeatedly over several rows</u>. First, the knitter needs to analyze whether an increase was repeatedly forgotten or if too many decreases were worked. Then the knitter should decide if the errors are acceptable to keep or if they should be corrected. Should the knitter wish to fix the issue, the simplest way to do this is to rip back to before the error started once the accidental increase has been located.

There are not enough stitches at the end of a repeat.
This could be due to an extra decrease or a forgotten
increase from the previous row. The knitter should
carefully compare the repeat to the pattern to ensure no
stitches were missed, then analyze the previous row(s)
in the same way until the issue is found. Once the error
has been located, the knitter can choose to either add
increases at the end of the repeat to fix the stitch count
or go back to the source of the error and correct it there.
It may be necessary to rip back to the problem or
perhaps it can be fixed by dropping a stitch or two down
then working them up the correct way (as described in
the previous the Fixing Dropped Stitches section).

Fixing Tight Stitches

Common Scenarios:

"My stitches are too difficult to slide up/down the
needles"

"I'm using the pattern's gauge yarn and needles, but my
stitches are too small"

Tension on the working yarn affects how tight the
resulting stitches will be once they have been worked.
Tight tension leads to tight gauge and tight stitches.
Tight stitches may be more difficult to slide up and
down the needles while being worked; they will also
result in smaller stitches which means more stitches per
inch. If all the stitches have been tight and there are
more stitches per inch than the gauge requires (if gauge
is necessary), the project may need to be restarted. A
second cast on with a looser tension will help set the

feeling for the following rows. If gauge is not important and the issue lies in a struggle to slide the stitches, simply moving forward with a looser tension should help on the following rows.

Fixing Holes Between Stitches

Common Scenarios:

"I have an accidental Yarn Over"

"My stitches are too loose"

"I haven't dropped a stitch, but there is a ladder forming"

Finding holes in a project is an inevitable part of knitting. Most beginners will accidently throw a Yarn Over or two while learning, typically getting the order of executing a stitch backwards. Other times holes might appear is if the tension is too loose, stitches will sag from the lack of support around them. Accidental Yarn Overs can be dropped on the round above with the "extra" slack being picked up by the surrounding stitches as more rows are worked. Laddering between Double Pointed Needles is another sign that the tension is not tight enough. Simply pulling tighter on the first stitch is not enough to correct laddering, however. Pulling tighter for the first three or four stitches will be necessary to fix and prevent laddering on subsequent rows. When it comes to loose stitches, a tapestry needle is exceedingly helpful. A knitter can use the tapestry needle to pull the Purl bump tighter then go methodically down the row pulling each sequential stitch tighter but not quite as tight as the first one to distribute the slack. The last potential option for fixing a hole is to take a length of waste yarn (preferably the same type/color as the yarn used in the project) and sewing up the hole with a tapestry needle.

Tip #33: Frogging is usually a last resort for knitters, however, the more it is done, the less it hurts.

Sometimes, the best path forward is to rip out early rather than forging ahead when something is clearly wrong. It is generally acknowledged that one should not continue intentionally with a mistake simply because a significant amount of time was invested in making it. Many knitters have frustrated themselves by attempting to continue only to have an issue get worse, or by attempting to fix a problem in place and make the whole mess bigger. If a knitter is not confident they will be able to fix a mistake, as painful as it might be, the most efficient option will be to rip back to before the mistake.

Review

- Learning to read the stitches is crucial to troubleshooting issues
- Some errors can be fixed from the row(s) above.
- Ripping out rows may be required to fix continual errors.
- Dropped stitches can be fixed using either needles or a crochet hook.

- Missed increases can be picked up the following row.
- Missed decreases can be worked either on the following row or by picking up from the previous row.
- Too many stitches can be fixed using additional decreases.
- Too few stitches can be fixed using additional increases.
- Tight stitches should be adjusted on following rows using looser tension.
- Holes can be fixed either with decreases or a tapestry needle and waste yarn of the same color.

Chapter 12: Other Types of Projects and Techniques

The projects and patterns covered by previous chapters are only a small sample of what is available to the interested knitter. Some knitters work all their projects from memory and have no need for patterns except for suggested guidance, while others knit from patterns by following every instruction to the letter. Still other knitters use a combination of memorization and pattern instruction, especially with new projects and techniques. Though only a few types of patterns and methods were used in previous chapters, that should not dissuade new knitters from exploring other project options.

Tip #34: There is always something different to learn with knitting. Whether it's new techniques or simply a new stitch texture, it would take more than a lifetime to learn "everything".

Shawls and Wraps

The triangle shawl has been a wardrobe staple for decades. Knitters are responsible for continuing this trend into the New Millennium. A light project, perfect for covering up cold shoulders in a chilly office or tossing on to ward off the fall air on the way to the mailbox, shawls are a perfect canvas for textures, colors, and lace alike. Wraps are shawls larger counterparts. Some wraps are square, rectangular, polyhedral, or even circular. The options for shawls and wraps are only limited by the imagination of designers. Variations on those patterns are limited only by the number of people who knit them; each project from a pattern is unique no matter how ardently a the knitter follows instructions.

Sweaters

Cozy sweaters are a classic knitting project. Almost everyone has either owned, or heard secondhand from those people, a scratchy sweater knit by a elderly relative. That is the stereotype about knitters and handknit sweaters. Knitters are elderly and sweaters are scratchy. Neither of those can be further from the truth. Knitters come in all ages, sizes, genders, nationalities, and ethnicities. Sweaters come in just as many variations as there are knitters, and yarn is a lot softer now than it used to be.

Cardigans

Cardigans are sweaters that open in the front. They can be long or short sleeved, have buttons or zippers to fasten them closed, or they can hang open. Cardigans can be knit top to bottom with set in sleeves, they can also be knit from the bottom to the top with sleeves that are sewn on, or any combination of construction techniques. Some knitters will work their cardigans in the round then cut, yes **CUT**, up the center of the front to place a zipper. This technique is called "Steeking" and though it may sound scary, it can also be quite satisfying.

Pullovers

Pullovers are sweaters that do exactly what their name suggests: pull over the wearer's head. While typically knit in the round, creative knitters can knit pullovers flat and sew up the seams later if they are aiming for a particular look on the sweater. One popular technique to combine with pullovers is colorwork, especially for the yoke of the sweater. The yoke is where the collar ends and increases for the shoulders/arms begin and end. Once it is time to separate the sleeves from the body, that is also when the colorwork for the yoke is finished and the body is knit. The reason for only doing colorwork in the yoke of a pullover is twofold: gauge is less important in this area and it is a style inspired by Icelandic sweaters.

Brioche

Brioche is a stitch that takes some knitters, even experienced ones, a long time to attempt. However, it is a pleasant stitch once the learning curve is overcome and results in a deliciously squishy rib-looking stitch. Brioche can be done with one color or two and when using two colors the stitch produces a stark contrast between the colors that is highly enjoyable. This stretchy stitch uses a combination of Knits, Purls, Slipped Stitches, and Yarn Overs in a two-row repeat over an even number of stitches.

Colorwork

Technically, knitting with more than one color can be considered colorwork. Most knitters and designers, however, use the term to refer to one of two main techniques. Some colorwork can range from two colors up to ten or more, depending on how adventurous the knitter decides to get. One way that knitters keep their different colored yarns organized is using spools. By placing small amounts of each color yarn on different spools, it is easier to keep track of and separate as they work.

Stranded

Stranded colorwork projects are knit almost exclusively in Stockinette, with the unused "floats" of yarn carried in the back on the wrong side of the work. There are a variety of ways to knit stranded colorwork, two yarns on one finger, one yarn on each hand and knitting both English and Continental at the same time, using a special ring to hold each color, or even utilizing a Portuguese knitting broach. Gauge can be difficult to maintain in stranded colorwork because the floats become another variable. Tight floats can result in clustered stitches and it is exceedingly difficult to fix them after the fact, nearly impossible. Loose floats will result in separated stitches, laddering, and holes. Stranded colorwork is not for the faint of heart or those who are not monogamous with their tension.

Double Knitting

This form of colorwork is two sides knit together simultaneously. Usually knit in two colors, one side is a negative image of the other. Similar to knitting in the round, the wrong side is on the inside, though these projects are typically worked flat. There are beautiful double-knit scarf and blanket patterns, even dishcloths and potholders can look fantastic when they are double knit. On the needles, there are twice as many stitches than there would be for a single knitted item because half the stitches are for the front and half are for the back. As a result, there are many Knits and Purls in both colors despite being knitted flat in Stockinette. The front stitches are the Knits, the back stitches are the Purls, and the results are all gorgeous.

Tip #35: Double knitting is an easy introduction to colorwork because the Knit and Purl alternate colors on the needle. The front is one color, and the back is another, until the design starts coming into play.

Finding new patterns, yarn options, techniques, and stitches are all part of the fun of learning to knit. Once the basics are mastered, the options open to what can be created with yarn. If something does not turn as well as planned, many knitters will pull the yarn out and re-use it in another project. Knitting gifts for holidays and birthdays is another way that knitters try new patterns they may not choose for themselves. Depending on the yarn choice and time invested, the resulting gift may not be the "cheapest" option, but handmade gifts are priceless to the recipient.

Review

- Shawls and wraps can be nearly any shape and have been around for hundreds of years.
- Sweaters can be as simple or as complicated as the knitter wants.
- Brioche has a learning curve but results in a fun and squishy ribbing.
- Colorwork takes some organization to keep from getting tangled.
- Learning new skills and techniques is fun.

Chapter 13: Frequently Asked Questions

Most knitters are happy to answer any and all questions someone may have about knitting. For the most part, the fiber community is filled with friendly, caring people who are eager to talk about the things they make. Nearly everyone in the community will enthusiastically share their passion with others, either in knitting groups, online, or by teaching their friends, family, co-workers, significant others, or anyone who will listen. While many common questions are listed in this chapter, new knitters should feel empowered to reach out to experienced knitters when the answers to their questions are difficult to find. The art of knitting has not been passed down through generations upon generations by keeping secrets and skills to one's self.

General Questions

Help! I stopped in the middle of a row; how can I tell which direction to go in now?

Sometimes, often for reasons outside our control, we stop knitting before we get to the end of a row. When knitting in the round, there really is only one direction to go (unless you're working on the short row heel of a sock). When you're knitting flat, however, can you be sure to keep working the same direction or are you doomed to guess and hope you're right? Take a good look at your stitches and compare them with the pattern. Were you working Knit stitches or Purl stitches? If you were working Knit stitches, or many other stitches, the working yarn should be coming from the back of the last stitch on the right side. For Purl stitches, the working yarn will be coming out of the front of the stitch on the right side.

My first several rows of knitting always look awful, is this common?

Yes! A single stitch in knitting relies on the eight stitches surrounding it for support and tension. At the beginning of a project, this support is just starting to take hold and as a result stitches or whole rows can look messier than expected. This occurs even with experienced knitters and is not necessarily a reflection of a new knitter's inexperience, it is how the mechanics of the stitches work. Try not to worry too much about appearance during those first rows, however, if there isn't gradual change as you work then some adjustment (such as different needles) may be necessary.

Are there any decreases that don't lean left or right?

To answer the question of whether there are decreases that don't lean, a bit more explanation on the nature of decreases is required. A single decrease results in one stitch being "removed", a double (or triple) decrease is the result of two stitches being "removed". Single decreases will always have a slant to them, that is simply a structural mechanic in the same way Knit stitches have the Purl bump land in the back. Decreases that combine three or more stitches can either have a slant to them or a prominent vertical stitch hiding the slanted stitches. A K3TOG or SSSK decrease will still lean in the direction of their two-stitch counterparts. There are two variations on the vertical stitch double decrease. The first is known as S2KP, which breaks down into Slip 2 together knit-wise, Knit 1, Pass the two slipped stitches over the Knit stitch. **S2KP** is also abbreviated as S2TOG-K1-PSSO (Pass Slipped Stitch[es] Over). The second variation of this double decrease is the **SK2P** and the difference here is rather than slipping two stitches, only one stitch is slipped then a K2TOG is worked. The SK2P is worked as a Slip 1, Knit 2 Together, Pass the slipped stitch over the K2TOG, or abbreviated as S1, K2TOG, PSSO.

Are Knitting kits worth it?

Whether knitting kits are considered "worth it" will depend on the knitter and what they are looking for in a project. Some retailers that sell knitting kits will offer a discount on the yarn if purchased through a kit, which may be enticing to the frugal knitter. Kits can be a convenient way of getting exactly the right amount and type of yarn for a particular pattern without having to shop around. However, some retailers will attempt to unload their hard-to-sell stock by packaging it as a kit. If you're thinking about purchasing a knitting kit for yourself, pay attention to whether it contains a pattern or not, whether you like ALL of the yarn included, and if any additional notions will be required that may be sold separately. If you're considering buying a kit for someone else, ensure that it is yarn they will like (some knitters have fiber preferences like "Absolutely NO Alpaca yarn please!") in their preferred color palette.

Can knitting needles be taken on airplanes?

It is always advisable to check with your local agencies with regards to what is allowed on flights. The United States currently allows knitting needles of all types aboard planes and the Transportation Security Administration (TSA) will allow them through security checkpoints with little to no issues. It is possible that other countries, or even smaller airports within the U.S., have tighter restrictions which is why verifying before a trip is recommended.

How is knitting different from weaving?

At their most basic, knitting and weaving create fabrics using different geometry. Weaving uses a grid of straight lines where knitting uses a series of loops. The tools required are vastly different as well; weaving utilizes a loom as a base for the fabric in progress where knitting uses anywhere from 2 to 5 needles. Knitting can easily be accomplished alone and is highly portable, whereas weaving requires smaller looms in order to be portable and weavers' results can be limited by the size of the loom.

Why does my knitting curl?

There you are, happily knitting along in the round or working Stockinette back and forth on straight needles, when inexplicably the edges begin to curl up on themselves. Your tension is good, your gauge is exactly what is required, even your stitches are straight (nothing dropped or added!), so why is this happening? Some stitch patterns can cause their fabric to curl— Stockinette is notorious for this—due to the way the stitches are worked and how they sit. When all the Purl bumps are on one side of the fabric, they slowly start to push against each other outwards, causing the edges to curl. This can be avoided by adding a border of some kind, usually Garter Stitch or Seed Stitch, to the edges or potentially blocking the curl out after the Bind Off.

Why is knitting so expensive?

Knitting can be as inexpensive or expensive as you make it. The large, chain craft stores will carry exactly what any knitter needs to get started at reasonable prices. Some knitters have been known to buy enough yarn for an entire sweater at a chain store at a cost of $5 (USD). Knitting will get more expensive when purchasing tools and yarn of higher quality than what is mass produced for chain stores. This is true of any hobby from sewing to baking to fishing; better tools and materials just cost more. There are yarn and tool companies that control their own production and distribution, which brings their overhead and prices down. If you would like the most "bang for your buck" buying from independent dyers and local yarn stores will support small business owners. These are people who will gladly assist or answer any questions you may have about their product or even general knitting issues—something that the large chain stores likely won't be able to offer.

What is "Yarn Bombing"?

If you've ever been walking down the street and came across a tree or fencing with what looks like a sweater or cozy on it, then it was Yarn Bombed. Yarn Bombing is the practice of guerrilla knitting pieces for or on public installations from trees to lampposts to statues. It is an act of both art and rebellion, though significantly less damaging than say graffiti. This unique action is generally done with the intent to envelope the community in a sense of comfort. Knitting comes from the heart and gifting that knitting to another person is an act of love. Yarn Bombing, usually, is done as an act of love for one's community. The next time you see a tree in a cozy or a statue in a sweater, know that someone did it to say "I give you, my community, this piece of me because you are worth it."

How do you decrease on Purl rows?

While the most common, basic stitches were covered in previous chapters, there may be an occasion where it's necessary to decrease on a Purl row and the K2TOG/SSK just won't cut it. That is where the P2TOG comes in: Purl 2 Together. It is executed the same way as a K2TOG but as if the knitter is working two Purl stitches. Practicing on a swatch would be a great way to see this decrease in action, how it looks when you're working it and when it's finished. Decide for yourself whether you'd like to do the P2TOG or if a K2TOG will suit your needs. It is your project and ultimately you are the one who should be happy with it.

What about socks? Are they difficult to knit?

Socks are not difficult at all! In fact, HowExpert carries another book specifically about knitting socks for the first time or improving your sock knitting skills. Check out "HowExpert Guide to Knitting Socks: 101 Tips to Learn How to Knit Socks and Become Better at Sock Knitting" on Amazon today! There is no need to be intimidated by knitting socks; we'll be with you every step of the way.

What's the difference between Ripping and Frogging?

Occasionally, there will be mistakes in a project that cannot be fixed from the rows above and the only alternative is to "rip back" to the error. Ripping can consist of anywhere from one row to many rows and the term likely comes from other textile industries that have "seam rippers". Frogging a project is when the knitter rips it all the way out, and the term is very knitter centric. When one is ripping a project out row by row, they rip it, rip it rip it, and spoken aloud this can sound like "ribbit, ribbit, ribbit", and thus we have the term Frogging.

How do I know if I need to Rip or Frog a project?

Ripping rows back or Frogging a project entirely is frequently a painful and difficult choice that is not taken lightly. Often, the rows ripped, or projects Frogged are the result of hours of work on the knitter's part. Seeing the kinked yarn spooling as it's ripped is frustrating and disappointing. Ripping is usually done to go back and correct a mistake where Frogging is done when the knitter is not satisfied with finished project. They may not be satisfied for a number of reasons, it does not fit the way it was intended, the yarn is needed for another project (common during World War II when supplies were scarce), or they simply don't like it. Giving yarn a new life in another project is almost always better than simply throwing out a garment.

Yarn Questions

Are yarn and wool the same thing?

If yarn is to a knitter as paint is to a painter, the difference in types of yarn is equivalent to the different types of paint. Acrylic, oil based, watercolor, gouache, and encaustic are all different types of paints made up of different types of materials. Painters use the appropriate paint for the canvas they're using or effect they want to convey. Knitters have a wide variety of yarn fibers where wool is one of many options. There are acrylic yarns, wool, Alpaca, silk, wool-nylon blends (for socks!), cotton, bamboo, and many others. Even among wool yarns there is tremendous variation depending on the breed of sheep and the way the yarn is spun from the fleece. Some of the wool variants include Merino, Shetland, and Blue Faced Leicester (affectionately shortened to BFL).

Tip #36: Alpaca fiber is both water and flame resistant!

Can yarn get wet?

Yarn can and should get wet, especially when being cleaned. The type of yarn, however, is what determines the temperature of the water and level of friction that it can withstand. Cotton and acrylic yarns can easily go through the washing machine and dryer without shrinking or loosing their shape. Wool yarns that are chemically treated to go through the washing machine are called "superwash" and even with that treatment, they should still air dry. Wool and other animal fiber yarns that are not listed as superwash should be washed in cold or lukewarm water by hand and air dried. Heat and friction will cause most animal fiber yarns to felt. This is where the fabric shrinks and starts to look almost solid, the fibers of the yarn blend together and the stitches are nearly erased.

What does Ply mean?

Tip #37: Throwers will slightly twist the yarn clockwise and untwist the ply.

Yarn is made up of one or more plies. A ply is a single strand of spun yarn, multiple plies spun together (or plied together) makes up a multi-ply yarn. When yarns are plied, they will be spun in the opposite direction the individual plies were spun. The reason they must be plied in opposite directions is when plies are made, the action of spinning them adds energy to the yarn. Counterbalancing that energy will allow the resulting yarn to rest in a more neutral state. If plies were spun clockwise and then plied together clockwise again, the resulting yarn would twist upon itself and be more difficult to work.

Tip #38: Pickers will slightly twist the yarn counterclockwise and tighten the ply.

What kind of yarn can be dyed?

Any yarn made from natural fibers (plant or animal) can be easily dyed. The type of dye and method used will depend on the specific fiber. Man-made yarns such as acrylic are not easily dyed. Acrylic yarns are spun from polymers that were the designated color prior to becoming yarn. Dying natural fibers can be easy and fun, there is even a method using a childhood favorite powdered fruit drink (unsweetened) and a slow cooker. This method, however, will only work with animal fibers as plant fibers require a different dye technique.

Can yarn be recycled?

Not only can yarn be recycled in several different ways, but there is yarn available for sale from a few retailers that is made from recycled materials. Some ways that other knitters recycle their yarn (especially snipped ends or tails) is by leaving the natural fibers out for animals to make nests with, stuffing for smaller projects, or by simply tossing them in their local recycling bins (as county/city rules allow). One retailer who sells yarn from recycled materials is Wool and The Gang that has a line of yarn milled from t-shirt fabric scraps from a factory in Turkey. Other companies recycle plastic bottles and different natural fibers for upcycled yarns.

What kind of yarn can shrink?

When it comes to washing projects, lukewarm or cool water is key. The temperature can be increased if the project is made of yarn where the base is cellulose—plant fiber. Bamboo, linen, and cotton are examples of plant-based yarn that will not noticeably shrink. Acrylic yarns are another example of non-shrinking yarns. The polymers used to spin the yarn do not have the same characteristics as natural fibers. Animal fibers, however, are on a bit more of a spectrum. Alpaca, or even Camel, individual fibers are long and thin like hair, which make them less prone to shrinking. Nearly all wool, except for Superwash, will shrink to some degree in warm water. Merino wool is especially notorious for shrinking by as much as 20% overall.

Will acrylic yarn melt? Would it be ok in a hot car?

Acrylic and polyester yarns can melt; however, it takes a higher temperature than a hot car to melt it. Temperatures not hot enough to melt acrylic or polyester can still damage the fibers and care should be taken to choose the appropriate yarn for a project. Acrylic and polyester yarn as a trivet for hot pans may not melt, but it will become deformed and hardened over time. They, likewise, should never be used to pull anything directly out of a hot oven. Acrylic and polyester yarn's melting point is 320°F (160°C) whereas the flame point of cotton is 491°F (255°C) and wool is 1058°-1112°F (570°-600°C). If you're cooking anything on the stove or in the oven at or above 350°F, it will absolutely melt any acrylic or polyester yarn that touches it.

Can you make your own yarn?

If you have ever thought to yourself, "knitting isn't unusual enough, I want a weirder hobby" then, my friend, you will be excited to hear about spinning. Why let the yarn manufacturers have all the fun when you can buy your own fleece or roving and learn to spin your own yarn? Many crafters see knitting or crocheting as the "gateway" into spinning. You can start small, a drop spindle can be made with items you likely have at home, many beautiful, supported spindles are available online as well, or you can jump right in and take a class to learn to use the spinning wheel. Some retailers (such as Blue Moon Fiber Arts) will offer what they call "sheep to shoe" kits where crafters are encouraged to spin the roving into yarn, then knit the yarn into socks.

Tip #39: Most commercial yarns are spun clockwise and plied counterclockwise.

Blocking Questions

<u>What is Blocking?</u>

In theater, blocking is the placement of actors and their movements upon the stage. Similarly, with knitting, blocking is a method of shaping an almost-finished project. Although commercial yarns are spun clockwise and plied counterclockwise to balance them out, the yarns still retain some of that charged energy. Giving the project a soak in (cool or lukewarm) water will help relax the yarn and allow it to bloom or grow. Blocking after the yarn has been squeezed of excess water will help guide the project to setting into its final shape and size. Once blocked, some patterns, such as those which include lace, can come alive in a way they could not before.

Do I need to block every project?

Not every project needs to be blocked, in fact, some projects should NOT be blocked. Negative ease is a term used for a fabric or garment that measures smaller than the wearer's measurements but will stretch to accommodate. Projects where negative ease is the intended result likely do not need blocking. This would likely minimize or erase any negative ease that was worked into the project. If a ribbed hat were blocked, it could stretch out and become too big to wear comfortably. Positive ease is where the fabric or garment's measurements are larger than the wearer's. Blocking can be utilized to add positive ease to a garment that is a big snug.

What types of yarn can be blocked?

The types of yarns that take best to blocking are animal based and a few of the plant-based yarns. Acrylic and cotton yarns do not take well to blocking, although, they do well to maintain their shape as they are knit. These things should be considered when choosing these for a particular project. Things like hats, scarves, blankets can be made withy any variety of yarn safely without having to worry about blocking (in most cases).

What tools should I use to block?

Many knitters get creative with both their blocking tools as well as their blocking area. From clotheslines to drying racks to backs of chairs, anything that gives the project its desired shape is acceptable! If the project is a medium or small size, knitters will frequently stretch and pin it to interlocking foam tiles either on the floor or elevated surface. Blocking wires are long, thin, flexible wires that allow a knitter to feed it through the edges of their projects and result in beautifully straight lines.

Does blocking a sweater make it bigger?

Blocking a sweater can make it bigger if it is stretched during blocking. If a sweater is being washed and simply laid flat to dry, it should not stretch or get bigger. Often, designers will call for sweaters to be blocked to open lace work or relax color work to make it more visible. It is also possible to stretch specific areas of a sweater while leaving others to lie flat, such as if the arms are too tight but the body of the sweater fits as expected.

How do I block a large blanket?

The Shetland Islands in Scotland have a traditional knitted blanket called a "hap". Historically, these blankets have been blocked on large wooden frames, called Hap Stretchers, using pegs and twine. There are many tutorials online from crafty folks who have made their own Hap Stretchers, but that is not a realistic option for everyone. Ideally, the blanket should be laid flat in an area with a lot of airflow (fans can help!). If there is not floorspace available, industrious knitters have utilized the tops of beds by laying down towels or even shower curtains to keep the bed itself dry.

Should I weave in ends before or after blocking?

Whether ends are weaved in before or after blocking is a personal decision for every knitter. Some knitters would like to have their project as soon as its dry from blocking, so their ends are woven in and snipped ahead of time. Other knitters prefer to wait until after blocking so that the ends will not pull or come loose as the project is pinned into place. Swatches can also be blocked to see how the yarn will respond and this can help knitters decide when and how to weave in their ends.

Health Questions

Is knitting good for the brain?

Knitting and other repetitive crafts are not only good for the brain, but they are also good for blood pressure, stress relief, and anxiety relief. Knitting can help prevent Dementia and Alzheimer's as well as help with mood stabilization. Numerous studies (as well as thousands of anecdotes) have shown that knitting, crocheting, and other needle-related crafts have a myriad of health benefits that are not limited to just the brain.

Does knitting cause carpal tunnel syndrome?

Carpal tunnel, arthritis, and Repetitive Stress Injury (RSI) can be aggravated by knitting, yes, but knitting is not known for being the direct cause of these injuries. Knitting will build up the cartilage in the hands, causing them to become stronger, rather than breaking them down. Good posture, larger needles, lighter projects, setting time limits, and allowing sore hands to rest in warm water before/after a craft session will help ease pain from injuries.

Can knitting cause finger/hand/wrist/arm/elbow/shoulder pain?

New knitters may notice new pains in their fingers, hands, wrists, or elsewhere in their bodies after they start knitting. As with any new physical venture, stiffness and soreness can come with the territory. You'll want to be sure to take regular breaks and even stretch, especially as the amount of your knitting time increases. True knitting injuries are not common, but they do happen, especially during marathon knitting sessions if you're not careful. If you are noticing consistent pain in the same place during or after a knitting session, try adjusting your posture or the way you hold the needles. Some knitters tend to grip the needles very tightly, which will cause soreness in their hands, and relaxing will help to alleviate this issue. If any pain is causing you alarm, please don't hesitate to visit your doctor and get checked out; they may even be able to suggest adjustments as well.

Tip #40: Many knitting communities have a "sit and stitch" in person gathering to knit and socialize. Some communities even do this virtually through video chat platforms. These events are great opportunities to meet other local knitters and ask questions.

Knitting has the beautiful ability to connect people to each other over space and time. Books written by long deceased authors can connect to modern knitters and continue sharing knowledge. Family members can pass down their skills to new generations as their family members taught them. Passing down a trade skill continues a chain started in the past through to the future. Throughout history, knitting was a necessity for clothing and income. Today, fewer people rely on knitting for their income and more do it for the sheer joy it provides. A few lucky knitters can feel that connection to the past and future and bask in their place in history.

Review

- Knitting is for everyone; it can be as simple or as complicated as you want.
- If something seems intimidating, break it down into smaller pieces.
- When in doubt, swatch it out.
- All single decreases (decrease by 1 stitch) will slant left or right.
- Some double+ decreases (decrease by 2 or more) will not slant, others will.
- Yarn can get wet; heat and friction combined should be avoided.
- Not every project needs to be blocked.
- Not every yarn responds to being blocked.
- Knitting is good for your health but, like everything else, is best in moderation.

Appendix – Bonus Lace Pattern

Fan and Feather

If you have knitted a swatch in the Old Shale lace pattern and found it not quite to your liking, you may want to give Fan and Feather a try. Often confused with the Old Shale pattern, there are some similarities, but the result does look entirely different. This written pattern and chart can be substituted instead of Old Shale in the cowl pattern. The Cast On and Bind Off methods would remain the same.

Step 1: Using the Long Tail Cast On, cast on 126 stitches

Step 2: Being careful not to twist, place a marker, join in the round, and knit 2 rounds

Step 3: (Purl 1 round, Knit 1 round) three times

Step 4: Lace Pattern

*Knit 4 Together (K4TOG), YO, [K1, YO] five times, Knit 4 Together Through Back Loop (K4TOGTBL), P1, repeat from * around
Knit 1 round

Step 5: Work the Lace Pattern ten times

Step 6: (Purl 1 round, Knit 1 round) three times

Step 7: Bind off using Jeny's Surprisingly Stretchy Bind Off

The result will look less wavey (as Old Shale looked) and more stacked. Fan and Feather is a lovely alternative to Old Shale when venturing into lace knitting. The pattern itself has been around nearly as long and is just as classic. Both Old Shale and Fan and Feather can be incorporated into the other projects listed in this book if the correct multiples of stitches are used. Old Shale needs multiples of 14 stitches and Fan and Feather uses multiples of 18 stitches.

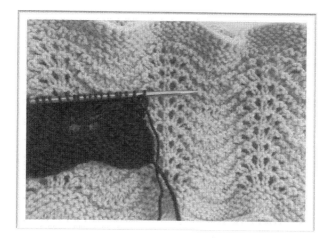

Glossary

DPN – Double Pointed Needle, a method to knit "in the round"

Magic Loop/Traveling Loop – another method to knit "in the round"

Judy's Magic Cast On – a seamless Cast On for toe up socks

Fish Lips Kiss Heel – a pattern for a short row heel by Sox Therapist, Ravelry.com

LYS – Local Yarn Shop

BFL – Bluefaced Leicester

FO – Finished Object

MC – Main Color

CC – Contrast Color

Stitch Abbreviations:

CO – Cast On

K – Knit

P - Purl

St(s) – Stitch(es)

KFB – Knit through the front and back legs of one stitch.

M1R – Make 1 Right by lifting the bar between the stitches from behind and knitting through the front loop.

M1L – Make 1 Left by lifting the bar between the stitches from the front and knitting through the back loop.

SSK – slip two stitches onto the right needle knit-wise and knit them together through the back loops.

K2TOG – Knit 2 together

P2TOG – Purl 2 Together

K4TOG – Knit 4 Together

K4TOGTBL – Knit 4 Together Through Back Loop

KTBL – Knit Through Back Loop

W&T – Wrap and Turn

About the Expert

Jeanne Torrey lives near Baltimore, Maryland, with her three kids, college BFF, and tuxedo cat. She has been knitting since 2010 and has knit more than 200 projects. You can find her on Ravelry.com under the username KnitsaTrap. When she's not knitting, Jeanne enjoys sewing, writing, and video games. She also practices the martial arts of Tae-Kwon-Do (currently a 2nd-degree black belt), Eskrima (green sash, Cacoy Doces Pares), and has recently started building her own gaming PC. Honorable mentions go to Jeanne's family for enabling her fiber habit, especially her mom, for providing proofreading support. This book is dedicated to Joey, Noah, and Leslie, who have appreciated every hand-knit gift Jeanne made them.

HowExpert publishes quick 'how to' guides on all topics from A to Z by everyday experts. Visit HowExpert.com to learn more.

Recommended Resources

- HowExpert.com – Quick 'How To' Guides on All Topics from A to Z by Everyday Experts.
- HowExpert.com/free – Free HowExpert Email Newsletter.
- HowExpert.com/books – HowExpert Books
- HowExpert.com/courses – HowExpert Courses
- HowExpert.com/clothing – HowExpert Clothing
- HowExpert.com/membership – HowExpert Membership Site
- HowExpert.com/affiliates – HowExpert Affiliate Program
- HowExpert.com/jobs – HowExpert Jobs
- HowExpert.com/writers – Write About Your #1 Passion/Knowledge/Expertise & Become a HowExpert Author.
- HowExpert.com/resources – Additional HowExpert Recommended Resources
- YouTube.com/HowExpert – Subscribe to HowExpert YouTube.
- Instagram.com/HowExpert – Follow HowExpert on Instagram.
- Facebook.com/HowExpert – Follow HowExpert on Facebook.

Printed in Great Britain
by Amazon